Angelo Maria Rinolfi

Angelo Maria Rinolfi

The Preacher

John Michael Hill, IC

Gracewing

First published in 2021 by
Gracewing
2 Southern Avenue
Leominster
Herefordshire HR6 0QF
United Kingdom
www.gracewing.co.uk

ISBN 978 085244 968 4

Typeset by Gracewing

Cover design by Bernardita Peña Hurtado

Cover image: St Marie's, Rugby. The parish church of the Rosminians in Rugby where Rinolfi lived as Provincial of the English Province.

CONTENTS

PREFACE

MOUNTAIN FOLK, it is said, make great missionaries. They possess a sort of rugged individualism and dogged perseverance which enables them to survive, indeed to thrive, in challenging circumstances far removed from the security of their native lands. Angelo Maria Rinolfi was one such, born in the far north of Italy, close to the Swiss border and to the great Alpine mountain chain. Every morning of his young life he would have seen the mighty massif of Monte Rosa, second only to Mont Blanc, looming to the north out of the morning mist and gleaming in the soft pink glow of low reflected sunshine. And he might have wondered what lay beyond.

Rinolfi was born of humble peasant stock into a very pious hardworking household. He was destined to become a Rosminian priest and to be sent after ordination on mission to the British Isles where he remained for the rest of his life. He was in character a quiet man, but quickly won the reputation of being a formidable preacher. He had a natural gift for languages, and his spoken and written English became perfect. He was given the task of being a missioner, conducting parish missions all over Britain and Ireland.

No other preacher at that time so touched the hungry hearts of vast congregations of people. Very many Protestants came into the Church as a result of his missions. Tens of thousands of cradle Catholics were moved by his preaching and persuasive eloquence. Their prayer and their sacramental lives were inspired to a new regularity and fervour, so that Catholicism in Britain grew from a few thousands in 1800 to around two million by the end of the century. The missions were a major cause of this revival. In Ireland too, the effects of centuries of persecution were reversed, and Catholics could again raise their heads with pride in their ancient faith.

Rinolfi preached nearly 200 of these missions over 25 years. He was a principal agent of this mighty change. Yet his name has been forgotten. He founded no institutions: no schools, no new parishes, or other charitable works bear his name. His influence was purely via the spoken word. People flocked to hear him; their hearts were changed and their lives enriched with a stronger, more vibrant faith. But such transformations are rarely graced with a written record.

Since Rinolfi was a very humble person and rarely spoke or wrote about himself, the sources for this book have been sparse. There is a very sketchy biography written a few years after his death by Fr Joseph Hirst. There are brief references in parish histories. There is a book published in Dublin in 1855, entitled *Missions in Ireland*. It is anonymous, but it is certainly Rinolfi's own work. He gave priority to work in Ireland, especially following the terrible famine of the 1840s. He was also acutely conscious of the centuries-long sufferings inflicted on the Irish by successive English governments.

The main sources of research for this book have been letters, diaries and reports kept in the Rosminian archives in Stresa. I am very grateful to the archivist Fr Alfredo Ceschi, sadly recently deceased, for his help and for the hospitality of the Rosminian communities both at the College in Stresa where the archives are kept, and in the Rosmini Centre nearby where the library contains a wealth of background material. My thanks are due to the Rector, Don Umberto Muratore and Frs Gianni Picenardi and Ludovico Gadaleta for their support. My friend Dr Samuele Tadini, a native of Stresa, has been an invaluable adviser, and translated the text into Italian for publication in Italy. He also introduced me to Professore Claudio Sagliaschi, historian of Prato Sesia, Rinolfi's birthplace, who graciously allowed me to interview him and presented me with his history of the town.

My special thanks go to Bishop Charles Drennan, an Ascribed Rosminian who read the text as it was produced; likewise to Mrs Margaret Greiff, another Ascribed Rosminian, who also read the text, helped me in finding sources, and wrote the Foreword. I am grateful for the support of my Rosminian brethren in my writing and for our Ascribed groups in New Zealand who have taken a steady interest in this work.

My old friend and artist Donald Moorhead drew the maps. Peter Elliott kindly supplied the photograph of Fr Angelo Rinolfi for the frontispiece of this book, and that of the interior of St Mary's, Newport. The photograph of Fr Luigi Gentili is from the Wortley Collection.

A final warm word of thanks to Tom Longford at Gracewing, the English publisher, for helping to steer the project. And to you, the readers, who are supporting me in recovering and celebrating the memory of a heroic figure from the past, whose name was lost and is now refound.

FOREWORD

WHEN I FIRST saw a photograph of a short-statured priest with what I read as a sympathetic round face, I was keen to discover who he was. Beyond finding that he was a Rosminian and his name was Angelo Maria Rinolfi, I found little mention of him in the standard books about the Institute of Charity, beyond the fact that he was a well-known missioner in England, Ireland and Scotland in the mid-19th century.

It was, therefore, a delight to discover that in the book now in your hands, Fr Michael Hill has amply extended my knowledge of Rinolfi's life, his deep personal piety and his sustained contribution to the Rosminians' great task of evangelisation in the United Kingdom and Ireland in the 19th century. At first, I had wondered what sources there would be since there was little in the way of published material to scour for details—or so I thought.

With his characteristic thoroughness, Fr Hill first went from New Zealand to Italy to spend time at Stresa, talking there to the guardians of the Institute's history and searching through the extensive archives for every mention of Rinolfi. The search was productive.

As with his earlier biography of Blessed Antonio Rosmini and his history of the Rosminian mission to Britain in the 19th century, Fr Hill takes pains to provide, in considerable detail, his subject's geographical and historical background. Here we begin in Novara, in the extreme north of Italy, and are given much illuminating detail about the problems and political uncertainties in Italy. These provided Rinolfi with a good grounding in being adaptable.

The Rinolfi family farmed and traded with modest success in this rugged region, and was able to send two of their sons, Angelo and Lorenzo, to train for the priesthood. By degrees, Angelo was drawn to embrace a religious vocation and in 1834 entered the Rosminian Noviciate at Monte Calvario, Domodossola. He probably never imagined that within a few years he would be sent to England. and furthermore, except for a few visits to Italy on Rosminian business, he would remain in the British Isles for the rest of his life. He was a very good linguist and few of those who heard him speak and preach in English took him for a foreigner.

An upbringing in beautiful but harsh surroundings, together with a thorough spiritual formation, gave Rinolfi a very solid grounding. His life would demand both physical and mental staying power to sustain his punishing regime of missions and retreats, let alone withstand the rigours of innumerable journeys on the slow early Victorian trains and down rutted Irish lanes. At every stage, his vocation required unstinted acceptance of the tasks assigned to him. He fulfilled all of them well.

Such virtues are rare and precious, the more so because Rinolfi did not seek to parade them. In him we have a wonderful example of Rosmini's *Maxims* prayed and lived: seeking without limit to please God, working peaceably for the increase of the Church and God's glory, abandonment to Divine Providence, the disregard of personal glory, and the application of intelligence to the performance of the tasks given him.

Angelo Maria Rinolfi, please pray for us

Margaret Greiff
Rosminian Ascribed

1

BEGINNINGS

IN OCTOBER 1837 two young Italians arrived by ferry at the port of Dover in southern England. They had just experienced their first ever sea crossing, coming across from France. They had been travelling for a week from the north of Italy, where they had previously been undergoing training to become Rosminian priests. Angelo Maria Rinolfi was aged 24 and was recently ordained. Fortunato Signini was even younger, being born in 1817 and still had a couple of years' study to complete before he too would be a priest. Neither knew more than a few words of English.

The pair were on their way to join a small Rosminian community in the city of Bath in south-west England. We have no account of what their first impressions were of their new home. Nothing could have been more different from the England of the early nineteenth century than the Italian state of Piedmont, where, in spite of the French Revolution, the way of life had changed little over the centuries.

Britain on the other hand was in the throes of the Industrial Revolution. Huge advances in science and technology had initiated the age of steam and steel. Railways were spreading fast across the English landscape. The great manufacturing towns and cities, especially in the Midlands and the north, were transforming Britain into the wealthiest country in the western world. At the same time there was a massive alteration in the distribution of population. Thousands were flocking into the cities to find work in the mines, mills and potteries, creating vast wealth, which largely went into the pockets of the ruling class.

The villages were being depopulated, and in the countryside there was widespread poverty; in the cities the workers were better paid, but they often dwelt in unhealthy slums breathing the smoke and pollution belched forth by the new factories. Rinolfi and Signini would in due course come to experience all this misery, and wonder what they had come to.

In fact, their immediate destination was the elegant city of Bath where the local Catholic bishop, Peter Baines, had established his seminary and a secondary boys' school adjacent to his home, the handsome Georgian mansion of Prior Park. Bath was the favourite watering place and retreat of the wealthy southern English, as readers of Jane Austen's novels will know. It was hardly typical of the new, commercially booming Britain.

The two young Italians arrived at Prior Park on 17 October having travelled across the south of England on top of a coach in thick fog. They were due for the next few years to live in a mansion presided over by a bishop with dangerous delusions of grandeur, teaching the sons of the rich who had little appetite for learning. It was not an encouraging prospect.

In time though they would come to move into the real Britain of bustling, dirty manufacturing towns, much poverty and squalid housing for the workers. There they would have to confront a Protestant ascendency contemptuous and hostile to Catholicism. Indeed they were both destined to spend the rest of their lives in the service of these people and of their masters: Signini as parish priest in south Wales and founder of the Rosminian parishes and schools in the capital city of Cardiff; Rinolfi as a missioner preaching all over Britain and Ireland. For them this was to be the true working out of their religious obedience.

2

EARLY LIFE

P RATO SESIA LIES in the province of Novara, in
north-west Italy. To the north at a distance of some
twenty miles looms the great *massif* of Monte Rosa, the
second highest mountain in the Alpine chain. From its flanks,
fed by melting snows, flows the river Sesia which winds its
way south through the Vallesesia, once an alpine lake, into the
mighty river Po and then eastward to the distant Adriatic Sea.
Prato Sesia means the 'meadow by the river Sesia': a poetic
name for this picturesque village.

Here, on 5 October 1813 was born Angelo Maria, fourth
son of Lorenzo Rinolfi and Lucia Franchi. There were also
three daughters and two younger sons to complete a typically
large peasant family. As he grew up one may imagine that
Angelo would have frequently gazed at the majestic, snow-clad
peak of Monte Rosa, looming to the north of the village, and
wondered what unexplored and mysterious lands lay beyond.
What sort of people lived there? Would he ever come to
experience that wider European world?

The earliest known inhabitants of this subalpine valley, in
the sixth century BC, were Celtic invaders from the north.
Because of the common origin of this population with the
Franks living north of the mountains, the area was known as
Cisalpine Gaul—meaning the part of Gaul on the south side of
the Alps. There could well have been further successive
movements of peoples from north of the Alps seeking a warmer
and more fertile land in which to live, and the Rinolfi family,
who had lived for several centuries in Prato Sesia, may have had

Celtic and Teutonic blood in their veins. Indeed the name 'Rinolfi' is thought to have come from the German 'Rainulfus'.

Angelo Maria's eldest brother Lorenzo, who became a priest of the local diocese of Novara, wrote:

> It has always been and still is a constant tradition in our family that the Rinolfis came from the north on occasion of the barbarian invasions of Italy. They have been settled for the last 200 or 300 years in the Vallesesia, at the village called Prato Sesia, between the borgo Romagnanosesia and Grignasco.
>
> So much is certain, as can be proved, the property deeds showing how our ancestors bought and sold land in this territory. They were engaged in farming and in trade, and with three pairs of oxen, used to supply the inhabitants of the Vallesesia and the Biellese with salt, tobacco and grain. Whilst engaged on one of these journeys, my great uncle Giuseppe, with his brother Mattia and nephew Bernardino in crossing the river Sesia, which was much swollen, perished in its waters.
>
> At 15 years of age my father was thus left head of the family. At the age of 20 he married a certain Lucia Franchi of Grignano, and had by her three daughters and six sons, of whom the fourth was your companion in Religion and my dearly beloved, don Angelo Maria.[1]

At the beginning of the nineteenth century the population of Prato Sesia was about one thousand. There were many small holdings of property and a few larger property owners, one of whom was the Genesi family who owned about 100,000 square metres of land. Three brothers of this family became priests: Giovanni Giacomo was rector of the parish for many years in the eighteenth century, and at the time of Angelo Maria's birth a younger brother, Angelo, was rector of the parish. It seems that at this brother's death all the family wealth went to a charitable trust, called the *Charity of the Holy Spirit*.

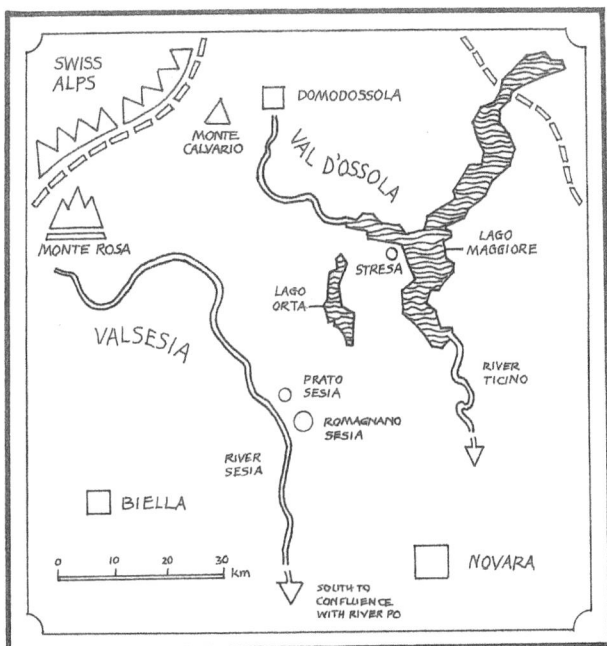

Map of area surrounding Prato Sesia

This was one of several such trusts, providing alms and other social services for the poor in the valley, who in our times would be provided for by the state. Even though the Rinolfi family was a large one they were able to provide a good basic education for Lorenzo and Angelo Maria—and perhaps others of the family—so that the two boys could progress to the local seminary for their priestly studies. They were probably assisted in this by these trusts.

In mediaeval times the valley was heavily wooded. Much of this abundant woodland was made available for poor families to collect firewood. Occasionally bears were seen but they disappeared long before Angelo's time. However, wolves were reported in the valley up to the nineteenth century, and in 1812 there was such an infestation of these animals that a

5

hunt was organised and generous rewards offered for the slaying of these beasts.

Progressively, some of the woodlands were cleared for cultivation, and at the same time ownership was transferred from a single landowner, a mediaeval Count, to many minor landowners. The redistribution of ownership proceeded more rapidly following the French Revolution. In 1800, roughly 30 percent of the land belonged to large landowners such as the Genesi brothers; another 30 percent was common land—woodland or heath available for grazing sheep; some land was owned by the charitable confraternities previously mentioned; the rest was small holdings held by peasant families such as the Rinolfis.

During the 1700s, agriculture had developed and flourished in this fertile valley. The river Sesia flowing through the village provided abundant irrigation as well as power to drive mills for the grinding of corn. This area of northern Italy, in the foothills of the Alpine chain, is noted for 'the fertility of the soil, the abundance of water for irrigation, and the fruit of many generations of productive labour … the *contadini* work the land more like gardeners than farmers'.[2]

Although corn for bread and pasta, maize for polenta, and rice in the paddies near the river were originally the chief crops, many others were developed. For instance quite a lot of hemp was grown for fibre: hemp to be spun into hessian or coarse cloth. And lots of nuts were grown, and indeed the valley became known as 'the land of the nuts'. Vines were planted extensively during the eighteenth and nineteenth centuries. The wine was mostly for local consumption; cultivating vines was quite labour intensive. Finally, a silk industry was developed. 29 February 1748 is noted for the first planting of mulberry trees, which led progressively to the cultivation of silkworms and the development of quite a lucrative trade.

Farming is always labour intensive, so the Rinolfi boys grew up to be typically hard-working, both physically and at their studies. During times of peace the valley became prosperous, and this enabled the children to be given a good education. However, there was a period of agricultural depression in the early nineteenth century, due to increasing trade bringing in cheap imports. There were also the beginnings of some industrialisation.

Prior to 1800 the peaceful existence of the people of the valley was scarcely troubled by what happened in the cities of north of the Alps. However, the French Revolution brought about some changes, which swept through Europe like the coronavirus, even penetrating to little villages like Prato Sesia. For more than 100 years Piedmont had been independent with its own monarch and government in Turin, while Lombardy and the Veneto were ruled by Austria. All this was altered in 1796 by the lightning campaign of Napoleon Bonaparte, who conquered Piedmont and then drove the Austrian army back almost to the gates of Vienna. Napoleon himself negotiated the peace, which gave France rule over the Veneto and Lombardy, previously under Austrian rule.

In 1800 Italy was still little more than a geographical expression, divided into some eight separate states, from Piedmont in the north to the kingdom of Sicily in the south. The Papal States, under the reactionary rule of the Popes straddled the centre of the peninsular. Soon, in Italy and right across Europe, the people felt the benefits of the *Code Napoleon*, a rationalisation of the laws and customs which controlled people's lives. Currencies and systems of weights and measures were decimalised. Napoleon improved the roads and communications system wherever his conquests led him. For example, a new road was built connecting the city of Milan with the Simplon Pass and Switzerland, and this road passed right through Stresa and Domodossola where Angelo would spend his years of formation as a Rosminian.

The catchcry *'liberty, equality, fraternity'* triggered off nationalist movements all over Europe—and this would have penetrated even into villages such as Prato Sesia. The people would have started to look beyond their immediate locality to the great cities such as Milan and Turin, and even beyond the Alps to Central Europe. In Italy this lifting of horizons eventually led to the unification of Italy and the creation of the modern Italian state.

Even today, love and loyalty to one's *paese,* or home town, is a strong feature of the Italian character, often fortified by religious feelings such as devotion to the local patron saint. But the influence of the French Revolution was to make ordinary Italians see their future as part of a much wider world. Indeed it would motivate many poor Italians to leave home and emigrate, especially to the New World.

One notable feature of Prato Sesia is the absence of a central piazza or market place, most unusual in Italy. Instead, the parish church and its surrounds seem to have been the heart of the village. The church is a noble and spacious classical-style building, recently restored. It is dedicated to St Bernard, who is reputed to have captured Satan and put him in chains! Inside there is a noble pulpit, and one may speculate that the young Angelo would have heard many an eloquent sermon, which may have been a source of his own extraordinary skill as a preacher. On one of the pillars separating the nave from the side aisle there is a plaque commemorating '*Angelo Maria Rinolfi*', as one of the distinguished sons of the village. He is described as a zealous missioner and preacher spending forty years in England and Ireland and being responsible for the conversion of many 'heretics' (*sic*) to the Catholic faith.

———◆◆◆———

Fr Joseph Hirst, an early biographer of Rinolfi, states that the northern Italians 'possess a robustness of character, a frankness of manner and a staying power'.[3] This laudatory judgment is confirmed in part by Élisée Reclus: 'The Piedmontese are,

generally speaking, possessed of a sober and steady tempera-
ment and are serious by nature. They are ingenious, industrious
and enterprising rather than imaginative. ... They respect
tradition and formality. They tend to be cheerful people'. This
encomium might well be a description of Angelo Rinolfi as an
adult, as others saw him; however, even as a small boy he
seems to have shown many of these character traits.

There are few sources describing Angelo as a child. The chief
source is his elder brother, the priest Lorenzo. Lorenzo tends
to eulogise his younger brother, who emerges from his comments like a plaster saint: 'he grew up in our little family circle
ever obedient to all, sweet-tempered, loving and pious, so that
we were wont to call him "angel" not only for name but also
for virtue'.[4] A much longer piece, composed probably to be
read by Angelo's Rosminian brethren after Angelo's death in
1877, states:

> Angelo ... always showed a strong inclination to piety
> and study. Having creditably brought his elementary
> studies to a close at home, always most obedient to his
> parents and anxious to imitate his brother Lawrence,
> already a cleric and then studying humanities, he begged
> the latter to instruct him in the rudiments of Latin ...
> In less than ten months, incredible as it may appear, he
> had mastered nearly the whole of the Latin grammar.

This extract suggests that Angelo already demonstrated that
gift for languages, which developed in his adult life and in the
course of time made him proficient in at least five languages.
Unfortunately there do not seem to be any surviving diaries
or documents regarding Angelo's early life apart from what
Lorenzo wrote. Anyway, even in his later writings Angelo
seldom if ever talks about himself. From them we can gather
a fair idea of what his subsequent career was, but what was
going on his heart and soul we can only surmise.

Lorenzo was attending St Charles' College in nearby Varellosesia as a philosophy student, and Angelo, aged 14, joined his elder brother there in 1827. Lorenzo observes:

> he soon distinguished himself by carrying off the prizes in humanities … By his good conduct he served as an excellent pattern to his companions, so that all his superiors without exception admired and loved him with special affection. When he donned the clerical habit, I cannot tell with what modesty and heartfelt joy he always assisted at the Church's sacred offices. Prayer, the frequenting of the sacraments, so entirely absorbed his energies that he became an object of universal admiration.[5]

Angelo appears from these lines to have been a serious and ardent student. In 1830 he was received into the Jesuit College in Novara, the centre of the diocese. He studied philosophy, but he also came to admire the way of life of the Jesuit Fathers, and this put into his mind the thought and ambition of following a religious vocation. He did not stay long there: in 1831 he moved on to the diocesan seminary to start theological studies, where he remained for three years. Lorenzo notes that his desire to follow a vocation to a religious Order grew stronger, and he came to the conclusion that he was out of place at the seminary. He needed to find a religious congregation, which would accept him.

Two powerful influences were to bear on this decision. First was a seminary friend who was nine months his senior. Carlo Narchialli was a native of the health resort of Tobello, not far from Prato Sesia. In April 1834 Narchialli left the seminary and went to Monte Calvario, Domodossola, to join the Institute of Charity. Angelo was even more swayed in his choice by the influence of Fr Giambattista Pagani, the spiritual director of the College. Pagani hailed from the town of Borgomanero, which is close to Prato Sesia. Although quite a young man—still in his late 20s—he had a profound influence on his students, showing qualities of spiritual leadership, which later made him an effective religious Superior. He too was about to change his state and move from the secular priesthood into the Rosminians.

A contemporary writer describes Pagani as 'attracting in a special way the esteem, reverence and affection of all by reason of his ardent and gentle piety, his great zeal and knowledge of the spiritual life, his discretion and competence in the direction of souls, accompanied with modest gravity, which was attractive because of his congenial manner'.[6] Pagani was greatly attracted to the spirituality of Antonio Rosmini, and would have communicated this to his students. It was only a few years previously, in February 1828, that Rosmini had founded a religious Congregation, the *Institute of Charity*, (later known as the Rosminians). His spiritual masterpiece, *Maxims of Spiritual Perfection*, had been published in 1830, and this would have been familiar to Pagani.

So, while the young Rinolfi was pursuing his studies for the priesthood, he was also reflecting and praying about the possibility of a religious vocation. Reading between the lines of his letters to his brother Lorenzo, it appears that their father was not at all happy at Angelo's choice. Angelo writes: 'a vocation known to be divine should be followed promptly … when the call comes from God, the flesh and self-love should be silent; father, mother, brothers, sisters, family are to be put aside; that the loving invitations of the Creator must be followed'.[7]

Angelo goes on to request Lorenzo to ask for their father's consent and blessing on his religious vocation. He sweetens his request by noting that if he were to follow Narchialli to Monte Calvario, then Lorenzo would be freed from the expense of maintaining him at the seminary. It had probably occurred to his father that by joining an active religious Order, Angelo might be sent to the other end of the earth and that the family might never see him again. That might have motivated his opposition. Indeed, that was what eventually happened.

———————●◆●◆●———————

Rinolfi arrived at the Rosminian novitiate at Monte Calvario, Domodossola on 5 November 1834. He made his first retreat under the direction of Fr Giacomo Molinari and was received into the novitiate on 21 November. At first the novitiate was housed at Monte Calvario, but in 1836 the novices were transferred to Stresa where a benefactor, Anna Maria Bolongaro, had given Rosmini a piece of land above the village.

A novitiate house was erected there, but the novices did not stay long, since later that year the Rosminians were given custody of the ancient abbey of San Michele on a mountain top in the Val di Chiusa near Turin. The novitiate was transferred to San Michele at the request of the Archbishop of Genoa, Cardinal Placido Maria Tadini: it was Tadini who had recommended the Institute of Charity to King Charles Albert of Savoy, the owner of the abbey. The site would certainly have been a solitary one. The nearest human beings would have been specks on the valley floor 1000 metres below.

On 23 May 1836 Angelo completed his novitiate there and made his first vows. Later that year he was ordained deacon at Gozzano. During all the time Rinolfi was a novice, Rosmini was seriously considering sending a group of his first companions on a mission to England. This was in response to an invitation of Bishop Peter Baines, Vicar Apostolic of the Western District of England. One of Rosmini's first companions, Fr Luigi Gentili, was chosen to be the leader of this mission. The Order had only been in existence a few years, yet already this bold outreach was becoming an exciting possibility. Indeed, when Rinolfi first arrived at Monte Calvario, he found that Gentili, in the words of Fr Hirst, 'could talk of nothing else'.[8]

The first trio were sent by Rosmini to England in 1835, to Prior Park, Bath, where Bishop Baines had established his base. Early in 1837 Fr Rosmini instructed the novice master Fr Francesco Puecher to interview the novices individually as to how they would feel about following Gentili on the English mission. Rinolfi was summoned, and Puecher graphically described the difficulties that would be faced: speaking a different language, having a different diet, facing the possibility of never returning to Italy. Rinolfi was left free to state his preference. We do not know precisely how he responded.

Early in April 1837 the two deacons, Narchialli and Rinolfi, went into retreat to prepare for ordination to the priesthood. This took place at Susa on 20 May. Rinolfi celebrated his first Mass on Sunday 28 May. In July the two newly ordained priests were summoned to Calvario to be interviewed by Rosmini, who was about to send reinforcements to England. In the event it was Pagani who was sent with another priest and three lay brothers. Rinolfi was sent to teach at the newly opened College in Domodossola, while Narchialli, who was delicate in health and was never seriously considered for the English mission, was retained by Rosmini as his secretary.

However, shortly afterwards Rinolfi was instructed to learn German as preparation for teaching it in England at Prior Park. He asked to spend time in the German-speaking part of the Tyrol, and spent some weeks at the Jesuit College in Brieg: he was determined to learn not only the language but also its correct accent. In October 1837, accompanied by the student Fortunato Signini, Angelo eventually set out for England. Both of them were destined to spend the remainder of their lives there.

NOTES

1   From Don Lorenzo's reply to the Rosminians written in 1892 in answer to an enquiry about the origins of his family.
2   According to the French geographer Élisée Reclus.
3   Hirst, J., *Words and Works of Father Rinolfi*, p. 6.
4   *Ibid.*, p. 8.
5   *Ibid.*, pp. 9–10.
6   Quoted by Domenico Mariani in *The Rosminian Generals and Bishops*, p. 16.
7   Letter to Lorenzo, 8 September 1834.
8   Hirst, *op. cit.*, p. 22.

3

PRIOR PARK AND LOUGHBOROUGH

R INOLFI AND SIGNINI arrived at Prior Park College in October 1837 in the fog. But after a good night's sleep, and the fog had lifted, they would have awoken to find themselves in a paradise. Prior Park mansion had been built in the Palladian style in the 1740s by the famous Bath architect John Wood the Elder. Superbly sited on the brow of a hill overlooking the ancient and elegant city of Bath, Prior Park was a magnificently conceived architectural ensemble stretching for a quarter of a mile across the hillside and comprising a porticoed mansion connected to flanking wings or pavilions by curved colonnades.

In 1829 it was bought by Bishop Baines to be the centre of his vicariate of the Western District, and with his customary vigour and imagination Baines set to work to create two colleges in the two pavilion wings. He turned the east wing, St Peter's, into a secondary school for boys, and the west wing, St Paul's, into a diocesan seminary for the training of future priests.

The small band of Rosminians had already been there for two years when the two newcomers arrived. Their zeal had transformed the place, especially regarding religious practice. Luigi Gentili had been appointed President of the seminary, where he taught the students philosophy. Another Rosminian, the Frenchman Antonio Rey, taught theology. At first the bishop was delighted with his new recruits, and he wrote to Rosmini that Gentili was 'a real treasure'.

He was not only Rector of the seminary but also spiritual director and director of studies for the whole establishment. Gentili set about the business of forming the young clerical students in the seminary not only to become spiritually mature but also to become as zealous for the conversion of England as he was himself. The President of the boys' school was a young Irish priest, Fr Moses Furlong, who as well as being a fine speaker, indeed an orator, was very devout and was greatly attracted to Gentili and to Rosminian spirituality. The following year he would apply to become a Rosminian, the first recruit to the Order in England.

Although the prospects for Prior Park appeared to be rosy there were serious problems. It was not easy to attract the fee-paying students, since they were competing with several other Catholic colleges for a very limited supply of boys. For this reason they drew many of their intake from Ireland. They were also short of staff. Some of the principal teachers fell out with the bishop and left.

The bishop again appealed to the Rosminians for help, and Rosmini sent them one of his leading priests, Fr Giambattista Pagani, and some brothers. Gentili was, however, dissatisfied with this, since Pagani was really only suited to teach in the seminary, and it was the school that needed staff. So Gentili specifically requested Rosmini to send Rinolfi and Signini, both of whom he knew to be capable of teaching in a school.

Rosmini had also sent his right-hand man, Fr Jean-Battiste Loewenbruck, travelling with Pagani to evaluate the English mission. Loewenbruck was full of praise for the work of the pioneers, especially Gentili for his spiritual leadership although he was critical of him as a teacher. But it was the bishop who came in for his most rigorous censure. The major problem at Prior Park, and it was intractable, was the personality of Bishop Baines, whom he described as:

very distinguished in many ways, but he is a swash-
buckler, a despot. He often acts on angry impulse, and
is capable of suddenly conceiving and executing
extreme measures that really require time to mature.[1]

Loewenbruck was very perceptive, and no doubt Gentili too
was aware of the bishop's shortcomings, but was very loyal to
him and utterly devoted to the work at Prior Park. What
Loewenbruck did not mention was that the extravagant
building programme had left Baines deeply in debt, and it was
probably this which finally led to his downfall and the failure
of Prior Park.

The college is set in the beautiful Somerset countryside, but
nearby Bath could not have been more untypical of the
England where the two young Italians had come to live. The
great manufacturing towns lay in the Midlands and the north
of England. Later on, both Signini and Rinolfi would have
plenty of experience of these towns, as well as of the magnificent new railway system which was spreading like a fast-
growing fungus all over Britain.

Nor would they yet know much about the great political and
social changes, then taking place in Britain. The redoubtable
Duke of Wellington was Prime Minister; his political companion
and successor was Sir Robert Peel, probably the most able Prime
Minister Britain has ever enjoyed. Wellington and Peel engi-
neered the process of Catholic Emancipation, which ushered
in a new era for Catholicism. It provided welcome relief from
persecution for the people and enabled missionary priests to
evangelise, and thus for the Church to grow.

Peel had an uncanny knack of finding good solutions for the
problems of his time, such as reorganising the civil service,
establishing a police force, reforming the prison system, and
transforming the chaos of a system of laws, which still officially
prescribed the death penalty for hundreds of petty offences. He
was capable of learning from mistakes and changing his mind.

Even though he was economically a liberal, Peel sought to find ways of ameliorating the lot of the poor. Ultimately he was driven from office because he brought about the abolition of the protectionist Corn Laws so as to guarantee cheap food for the masses.

But none of this would have had much direct impact on the daily lives of Signini and Rinolfi: for two young Italian schoolmasters the world of London and parliament was as remote as the moon. Their first experience in England was to be the humdrum routine of the classroom, mixing with lay teachers and parents some of whom were wary of the Italians and even hostile towards them. They had to get used to a new language and English ways, climate and diet. Rinolfi spent five years altogether at Prior Park, mostly teaching German and Italian. It was a painful, if necessary, period of learning. He was, as ever, uncomplaining; but reading between the lines it was not the happiest time of his life.

The good atmosphere at Prior Park was not destined to last. Some parents and staff brought pressure to bear on the bishop to rein in Gentili and limit the influence of the Italians. The English Church had been cut off from Continental influence and in particular from Rome for hundreds of years. Gentili, in a report written in 1839 to *Propaganda Fide* (the Vatican department for missionary lands) regarding the possibility of reinstating diocesan bishops in place of the system of Vicars Apostolic, described the English Catholic Church as 'Gallican'. This term was used to describe the French Church which for centuries claimed a certain independence of Rome and the Papacy. England had long rejoiced in a cosy isolation by reason of its distance from Rome and the prolonged time of persecution, and its leadership was in the hands of the wealthy Catholic aristocracy to whom the clergy were subservient. Rome and the Vatican—and no doubt some of these Italian religious practices—were almost an alien culture to the still somewhat closeted English Catholics.

What eventually transpired at Prior Park was that Bishop Baines ceased to be supportive of Gentili, and appointed a vice-Rector who undermined much of what the Rosminians had achieved. It seems that the bishop was particularly resentful that Moses Furlong, who had been with him at Prior Park from the beginning, had applied to join the Institute of Charity. Rosmini wrote to the bishop assuring him that Furlong, or any others who might wish to become Rosminians, would remain at Prior Park. Furthermore, Rosmini noted that unless the Institute started to recruit members in England it would never take root and be of lasting support to the English bishops.

However, Baines was not be moved, and at the end of 1838 he took Gentili away from the school and sent him to look after a convent of Religious Sisters at Spetisbury in Dorset, many miles away. Rosmini appointed Pagani as Superior in place of Gentili. In fact, this was a salutary move because although Pagani was no good as a teacher of boys, he was an excellent religious superior, and the little community settled down more harmoniously. Pagani himself often suffered from ill health and depression, and had to return to Italy a few times to recover. However, he grew to be more tolerant of England and the English than Gentili had ever been, and under his kindly rule the Institute in England was to progress in numbers and works.

In his letters to Rosmini, Pagani refers periodically to Rinolfi, whom he obviously trusted and admired. In November 1839 he writes:

> He [Rinolfi] is engaged in teaching German and Italian to a number of youths in both Colleges, with much patience and perseverance. A month ago he began to preach in English, in which he succeeds very well, both on account of his excellent pronunciation—in which he surpasses all the other brethren, whether Italian or French—and because he prepares and studies with great diligence. All the members of this establishment, whether ecclesiastics or seculars, have a high opinion

of him, and bear him much affection … priests like him who know their theology sufficiently well to preach the divine word solidly and with fruit, to administer the sacraments and to direct souls in the way of holiness, and who can speak and hear confessions in five languages, are very rare.[2]

He also describes him as 'a lover of order and of labour, devout and obedient'.[3] On another tack he writes to Rosmini on 18 May 1840:

It appears to me that Fr Rinolfi has especial aptitude for remarking on the failings of others, when he is charged with this duty. But he is full of charity; whence, of the defects observed and not merely imagined, he says nothing but to those concerned and only when a favourable opportunity offers: but with all others he keeps perfect silence.[4]

Teaching languages to reluctant children was especially burdensome. Pagani comments (*12 February 1841*):

Rinolfi bears with much patience the labours of his schools, which appear to me to be very heavy, he being one of the most burdened teachers of this establishment. Besides, this office is anything but agreeable to him on account of its monotony, and owing to the difficulty he finds in managing his pupils for the most part averse to study.[5]

Rosmini himself showed great interest in the progress of the English mission and wrote regularly to members of the Prior Park community. He appears as a great and wise leader presiding over this new mission from afar. The author of a life of Ambrose Phillipps (about whom we will hear again later) describes Rosmini as a 'farsighted and prophetic figure'. His letters are always encouraging, and the advice given is carefully adapted to the recipient.

For instance, to Gentili he tries to temper his zeal by urging him to be more prudent and restrained in imposing Italian ideas on the English. 'Be more magnanimous' he says, 'and don't be so absolute in what you say'. Gentili was obsessed with the evils of England and the shortcomings of the clergy. He took little notice of Rosmini's advice, although eventually with experience he came to moderate his censorious opinions. Pagani, who was inclined to be introspective and to become depressed, he tries to cheer up. For his retreat, Rosmini advises that he should meditate more on positive and encouraging things and less on his own failings.

To Rinolfi, Rosmini writes (16 March 1838):

> Be quite sure that God will bless your labours, and what is more, will reserve for you an abundant reward. … Do all that is within your power not only to strengthen yourself, and confirm yourself solidly in your holy vocation, but also to give constancy (as far as this depends on you) to your companions. The enterprise you are engaged in is great—all the greater because at present it may seem small and even fruitless. So you have to put all your trust in God and obtain from him greatness of heart, generosity and courage.[6]

Later, Rosmini responds to Rinolfi's difficulties in the class-room (23 August 1838):

> our defects and failings humble us all the time, but they must never discourage us. We have to say often: 'let God rise up, let his enemies be scattered', and other such expressions of confidence, of which the psalms are full. Stay at your post until obedience recalls you, and be certain that this is the will of God and the sure road to your sanctification.[7]

Rinolfi found comfort in Rosmini's words of pointed encouragement. Indeed, he stayed five years at his post—until 1842 when the last Rosminians were withdrawn from Prior Park.

The Frenchman Emilio Belisy, who had been there from the beginning, describes their departure:

> The establishment of Prior Park is magnificent, but it is overwhelmed with debts, which have fallen on the head of the dear Bishop. This distressing situation, out of which he will have difficulty extricating himself, would make us wish to continue to serve him for nothing, as we have done for the last seven years; but he and his priests want to be rid of us. Other bishops look on us with a more favourable eye, and receive us with open arms; it is to these we are going to serve.[8]

In fact, it was to the Midlands district that the Rosminians were to go, at the invitation of Bishop Thomas Walsh, the Vicar Apostolic. Walsh had recently set up his seminary at Oscott College, near Birmingham, under the leadership of Msgr Nicholas Wiseman (later to become the first Cardinal Archbishop of Westminster). The Midlands thus became the principal area of operations for the Rosminians in England, and has remained so ever since.

There was already one Rosminian in the Midlands district. Luigi Gentili had in 1840 gone there to be chaplain to Ambrose Phillipps, squire of Grace Dieu Manor situated in Charnwood Forest six miles from the market town of Loughborough. Phillipps had been converted to Catholicism at the age of 16. At 21 he visited Rome and met Gentili, then studying for the priesthood at the Irish College. Phillips was passionate about the conversion of England to Catholicism, and wanted Gentili to come to England after he was ordained, to evangelise the people on his estates. Phillips also went on to Domodossola and met Rosmini himself, who was much taken with the young man.

This first approach came to nothing, but Phillipps wrote again to Rosmini several years later with the same request. Gentili, who had finally left the jurisdiction of Bishop Baines, was now free to take up this new offer, so Rosmini agreed.

Gentili arrived at Grace Dieu in May 1840 and soon began making converts in the surrounding villages. Ambrose built chapels in two of these, Whitwick and Shepshed, which Gentili served, and also founded Catholic schools in the area.

In 1841 Bishop Walsh invited the Rosminians to accept the mission of Loughborough, close to Grace Dieu, and this became the first Rosminian parish in England. Loughborough was a small market town of about 10,000 inhabitants set in rolling agricultural countryside, but with only a tiny Catholic population. Pagani went there himself to be parish priest, and took with him Moses Furlong as assistant.

In 1842 Gentili had a serious disagreement with Phillipps, who summarily dismissed him from being chaplain. Phillipps tended to be as strong-minded and hot-headed as Gentili himself, so it was a wonder their partnership lasted as it did. However, this breach enabled Pagani to bring Gentili to join the community at Loughborough.

In fact, once he was away from Grace Dieu, Gentili soon re-established good relations with Phillipps, and later on they went together on a visit to Oxford University to meet the Tractarians, the leaders of the so-called Oxford Movement, which was bringing the Anglican Church closer to Catholicism. While there, Gentili and Phillipps met John Henry Newman, the leader of the Tractarians, who a few years afterwards was to become a Catholic himself. They also met a young disciple of his, William Lockhart, who later joined the Rosminians.

Meanwhile Rinolfi was soldiering on at Prior Park, until finally in July 1842 he and the other remaining brethren were withdrawn. Interestingly, many of the teachers at Prior Park petitioned for Rinolfi to stay on, since among all the Rosminians he was especially esteemed by the staff. However, Pagani, being well aware of Rinolfi's skill as a preacher, brought him to join the community at Loughborough. It was the end of his career as a schoolteacher. His experience at Prior Park, however, was by no means wasted: it helped give him confidence and skill when speaking English on his feet, to communicate easily and to express his ideas to his audience in clear and logical language.

Pagani returned once again to Italy, and Gentili succeeded him as parish priest of Loughborough. He launched himself with his customary zeal into this task, introducing Marian devotions and improving the singing and the furnishings in the church. He also established charitable organisations in support of the poor and founded a temperance society. The parish was spread over a wide area, and there was plenty of work for Rinolfi and the other priests of the community.

Two Rosminian sisters shortly arrived from Italy to establish a convent and school in the town. Furlong became their chaplain, and they too soon began to attract novices. So it was a scene of great pastoral activity.

About this time Gentili was visited by Newman's disciple, William Lockhart, who asked to do a retreat under him. Lockhart was so bowled over by this experience he at once requested to be received as a Catholic and join the Rosminians. It was providential that Rinolfi at this time got to know and work with both Furlong and Lockhart, who in later years became his companions as missioners.

Perhaps the most significant new initiative by Gentili, in March 1843, was to hold a parish mission. Rosmini had previously suggested parish missions to Gentili, and he was at last in a position to try in England what was a great instrument of evangelisation on the Continent. This was the first full parish mission ever to be preached in England—or indeed in the English language. Gentili was the leading preacher, with Furlong and Rinolfi assisting him.

An observer was Bishop John Briggs, Vicar Apostolic of the Northern District, who came down especially from York to sit in on it. The mission was hugely successful, attracting over fifty converts from Protestantism. Briggs was most impressed and persuaded Gentili to come north and give missions in Lancashire and Yorkshire. This was the start of a flourishing era of expansion for the Rosminians in Britain, since the Order became better known wherever the missions were held.

Over the next year or so, Gentili was frequently absent from the parish giving missions and retreats. In 1845 Rosmini appointed him full time to this work, with Moses Furlong as his companion. Rinolfi remained at Loughborough, and was chosen to succeed Gentili as parish priest.

NOTES

1 Leetham, C. R., *Luigi Gentili, p. 88.*

2 *Hirst, op. cit., p. 30.*

3 Letter, *27 February 1840.*

4 Hirst, *op. cit., p. 31.*

5 *Ibid.*

6 *The Ascetical Letters of Antonio Rosmini*, Vol. III, no. 50.

7 *Ibid.*, Vol. III, no. 61.

8 Hirst, *op. cit.*, p. 42.

4

PARISH PRIEST

THE PARISH OF Loughborough was widely spread, consisting not only of the town of Loughborough but also several outlying villages in all directions. In 1834, the church and presbytery had been built on the Ashby road. This road went west out of the town through the village of Shepshed and, a few miles further on, to Grace Dieu, the residence of Ambrose Phillipps. Later, the Rosminians were to acquire Grace Dieu and run it as a school, which it continued to be until recent times. Travelling still further west, you come to the old town of Ashby-de-la-Zouche.

Phillipps's property included a wooded park, a relic of the ancient Charnwood Forest, and to the south an area of wild upland crags, with rocky outcrops of pre-Cambrian granite, which geologists judge to be the oldest rocks in England. There he had established the monastery of Mount Saint Bernard's, run by Cistercian monks who came from Mount Melleray abbey in Ireland. The monks were attempting to support themselves by creating a farm on the wild moorland.

In 1843 Ambrose also erected a Calvary on one of the rocky slopes, with a life-size crucifix, and on 3 May, for the feast of the Finding of the Holy Cross, he invited Fr William Ullathorne, later Archbishop of Birmingham, to attend its opening. A good crowd from the surrounding villages, estimated at over 800 people, gathered along with three choirs for the occasion, which no doubt raised the locals' curiosity. Gentili, as parish priest, presided at the ceremony, accompanied by other Rosminians and a secular diocesan priest from the village of Whitwick, Fr Samuel Whitaker.

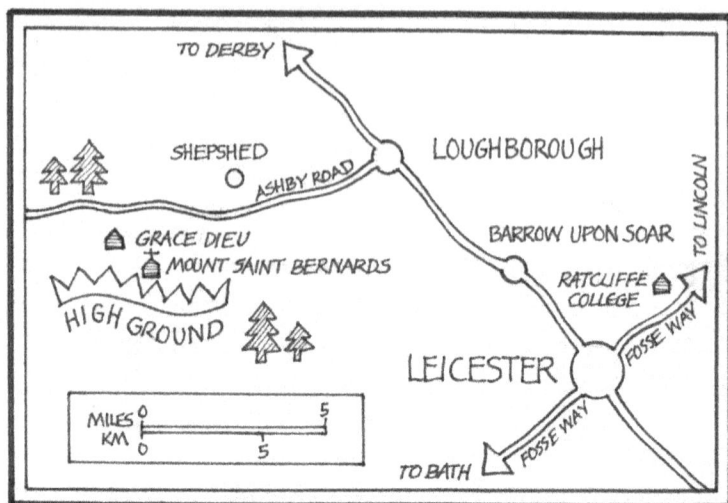

Leicestershire showing key points for Rosminians

This was a unique event. Such a spectacular open-air celebration, while not uncommon in Italy, had hardly ever been seen in England since the Reformation. Here is an extract from a contemporary account:

> Not a cloud was in the sky, and the young green of spring, lighted up by a brilliant sun, clothed the woods and hills in festive attire … an abrupt hill rises, studded with grey rocks, … This hill is backed by a dense wood of oak and fir, through which a winding path leads to Grace Dieu Manor. On a craggy rock, which forms the summit of the hill, stands a well-executed representation of our blessed Saviour on the Cross. The figure, nearly as large as life, was on this evening clearly defined against the bright blue sky, and this sacred image of man's redemption, seemed to stand forth in bold relief, as a cheering pledge of a revival of the ancient faith, of hope, and of charity, and of good-will to man …

> Three choirs from the Catholic Churches of Sheepeshed, Whitwick and Grace-Dieu, walked two

and two in surplices, each choir preceded by a cross-bearer bearing a magnificent processional Cross, each of which was different, and designed by the truly Catholic architect, the talented Pugin; then followed in surplices and robes, the Rev. Dr. Gentili, Superior of the Brothers of Charity … and the Rev. Angelo Rinolfi, another member of that institute; the Rev. Samuel Whitaker, parish priest of Whitwick … followed the Brothers of Charity, bearing a splendid reliquary, containing a portion of the HOLY CROSS …

When the procession had arrived at the foot of the Crucifix, the assembled people gradually assembled near the summit in various groups … Nature herself seemed hushed; not a breath of wind stirring when Dr Gentili, kneeling, intoned the *Veni Creator* in English, which was taken up by the choir and many of the crowd; he then mounted the step on the which the Cross was raised and addressed the people, … the attention of all was riveted [by] his clear explanations of the festival, of the veneration to be paid to relics, of the great atonement offered by the Cross for sin, of the duty by which every Christian is bound to embrace the Cross, and to carry the Cross. A no less eloquent sermon … followed, by the Rev. A. Rinolfi …

The whole was concluded by a scene which it is difficult to believe could have taken place in England, and which, aided by the wild rocky landscape, vividly recalled some religious festival in the Tyrol. Once more mounting the step of the Cross, Dr. Gentili held on high the reliquary, briefly recapitulating his previous explanations … and announcing the Benediction about to be pronounced to the assembled people … A dead silence prevailed when the soul-stirring preacher ceased to speak, and returned the reliquary into the hands of the parish priest, … and all simultaneously fell on their knees, bowing their heads; every hat was raised ... as the Rev. Mr. Whitaker gave the solemn Benediction with the Reliquary. Mr. A. L. Phillipps, his lady, and their guests, then ascended to the summit, and on their knees kissed the reliquary held by the priest; their example was followed by all, respectfully approaching one by one, till a countless number had fulfilled their anxious wish.[1]

While the occasion was remarkable, it was also typical of the more colourful popular devotions which the Rosminians introduced in their parishes. The above account includes the first mention of a sermon being preached by Rinolfi at Loughborough while he was assistant to Gentili. When Gentili was withdrawn to become a full-time missioner, Rinolfi succeeded as parish priest.

This new responsibility kept Rinolfi very busy: missionary labours in the neighbourhood, visiting his flock, and continual preaching fully occupied his time.[2] 'Sermons were preached every evening in the Loughborough chapel for nine days in preparation for Christmas 1843 and during the month of May 1844. Rinolfi preached every evening. Thus were two Italian customs successfully introduced'. Although Rosmini had counselled caution in imposing Italian customs, the success of this initiative could be seen in the numbers who attended. A latent spiritual desire among the people was at least being met.

On the east the parish extended to the village of Barrow-on-Soar. The river Soar was part of the extensive canal system spreading across England for the purpose of carrying merchandise. Fr Peter Hutton, another Rosminian recruit from Prior Park, reports visiting this village and describing a young woman convert whom he met when accompanying Rinolfi. 'Her very countenance beamed with inward joy and satisfaction which she derived from such society ... [but] she was subjected to a regular course of persecution from her bigoted relatives and neighbours'.[3] Hutton also refers to another young convert who was thrown out of her home because she had become a Catholic.

This form of persecution was not uncommon during the first years of Catholic evangelisation after Emancipation. Even in Loughborough there had been insulting behaviour towards the priests, and the Sisters had dirt thrown at them when they first walked in the streets. However, very soon the Rosminians, both priests and Sisters, earned the respect of the citizens, and the atmosphere became calmer. A visiting Rosminian was amazed that the priests went about the streets dressed in their soutanes, and were greeted respectfully by the people.

Protestants started regularly attending the Sunday evening services to listen to Rinolfi's sermons and to sing hymns. The flow of converts continued, as did the regular arrival of young men seeking a vocation to the religious life. Indeed, the house in Loughborough soon became inadequate to accommodate both the community and the novices as well as visitors. This prompted Pagani and Gentili to look around for a property to house prospective candidates, and a tract of land was bought some eight miles away from Loughborough towards the city of Leicester. It was given the name of a nearby village, Ratcliffe. A new college was designed by the celebrated architect Augustus Welby Pugin, and building went ahead quickly. It was decided to include a boys' school, as at Prior Park, since this was seen as a prime source of new vocations.

By this time the Institute of Charity was becoming well known throughout England, so that the Loughborough house attracted a steady stream of visitors, including several bishops and new converts such as John Henry Newman. They would often come to make a retreat under the direction of one of the three or so priests assigned to the house. Rinolfi and others were called upon also to go out and give retreats and missions.

Rinolfi gave retreats to the Sisters of Mercy in Nottingham and Birmingham, and to other communities of Religious also, as well as to the clergy of the Midlands district at Oscott. In May 1846 he preached a mission in Hinckley, outside Leicester, in the company of Moses Furlong. Thus he was being gradually prepared for what was to become his life's vocation as a missioner.

Rinolfi in Newport

In 1846 Luigi Gentili and Moses Furlong had preached a mission in the south Wales town of Newport, which was attended by the local bishop, the Benedictine Thomas Brown. The bishop was so impressed that he asked the Rosminians to come to Wales and take over the Newport mission. Hutton and Signini were first sent, but Hutton became ill and was soon moved back to Ratcliffe, where he flourished in a more academic atmosphere. Accordingly, in 1847 Rinolfi was moved from Loughborough to Newport to be parish priest, with Signini as assistant. This was the beginning of the Rosminian presence in south Wales, which continues to this day.

Newport was then the most important town in south Wales, having a rapidly growing population of about 18,000. It is situated on the river Usk where it joins the Severn estuary. At this time Cardiff, about 10 miles away further west, was still relatively insignificant. The discovery of coal further inland and the creation of deep-water ports caused both places to expand rapidly in population from 1840 onwards.

1847 was also the high point of the terrible potato famine in Ireland, and one of the consequences was the mass exodus of thousands of starving and diseased Irish, many of whom came across the Irish Sea to Britain. The chief places where they initially settled were Glasgow and Clydeside in Scotland, Liverpool in Lancashire, and the seaport towns of south Wales, mainly Newport and Swansea, and later Cardiff. The influx of these poverty stricken refugees put huge pressure on the local authorities—to feed them, house them and provide medical services.

Pagani describes the situation which the first Rosminians faced:

> The church [St Mary's] is in an unfinished state and is extremely cold in winter. Half the Catholics in Wales are attached to this town which is daily growing in importance … The congregation is very poor and may be said to be an Irish one of the lowest grade— drunken, ignorant and superstitious.
>
> I visited the fever hospital with Signini and saw dead, dying men, women and children all huddled together without curtains. What a scene! How to hear confessions, administer the sacraments? The yard is full of the hungry, half-starved, the weak and famished, craving charity. What can we do with our limited means?
>
> Widows wanting protection, women deserted by their husbands, and dreadful fights among the Irish on Sunday evenings, stabbing one another. Battles between the Irish and Welsh, coming to ask the priest to secure them bail. Whole streets of Irish not coming to Mass on Sundays. Men and women calling for the priest instead of the doctor to lay his blessed hands on parts of the body in the superstitious notion that this will cure their ailments.[4]

The deadly disease typhus, which was highly contagious, spread inevitably from the immigrants to the local population, and one of the casualties was Signini himself who had to be withdrawn for a time. Fortunately he recovered and eventually returned to perform long and faithful service to the new mission in Cardiff.

Though many of the Irish immigrants were themselves immune from the pestilence, they could still spread it, medical personnel and the priests who ministered to the refugees being especially vulnerable. (For instance, it caused the death of at least half a dozen priests in Liverpool, where the greatest concentration of Irish refugees was to be found.) This was the challenging scene which met Rinolfi when he arrived in Newport in September 1847.

Rinolfi was soon joined by another Italian, the newly ordained Domenico Cavalli. He was a very capable pastor and was to remain in Newport as parish priest for over forty years. His presence enabled Rinolfi to leave the parish and preach retreats and missions away from the town. In March 1849 he accompanied Fr Lockhart in giving a mission at the large parish of St George's Church (now Cathedral) in Southwark, south London. More often, however, as his reputation for preaching grew, he was increasingly called upon to give retreats: to convents and also to the Ratcliffe Rosminian community. Some retreats were also given to diocesan clergy: to the Midlands clergy at Oscott in July 1848, to York and the northern clergy at Ushaw College, Durham, later that month, and to the Lancashire clergy in August 1848.

Rosmini meanwhile continued from far away Italy, to guide his English brethren. In January 1847 he gives Rinolfi very practical advice about preaching missions the aim of which should be to increase the faith of participants:

> It will help you if you study carefully what difficulties exist in the minds and hearts of the people and tend to keep these brethren of ours divided from the Church. Then, when you know exactly and for certain what are the main ones, you will know how to frame your words and present your reasoning when it comes to speaking, whether in public sermons or in private conversations.

> At times it pays to speak briefly, in a way that hits the mark, rather than to go on at length in a vague and rambling manner. It is especially helpful if you confine

yourself to the great truths of the faith which are believed also by those you are faced with—such as love of and faith in Christ, charity, justice etc. Because these things act as seeds, which go on then to give rise to faith in other, more specialized matters. You have to keep on sowing, without expecting to reap at once—as our Lord himself did.[5]

In a letter to Fortunato Signini written at the same time, Rosmini uses the same metaphor of the seed, sown in the hearts of the people, which will bear fruit in time:

> I believe that you must be mostly concerned to get the people to understand the main obligations that the law of the Lord imposes, rather than speaking about matters of counsel or those concerning perfection … First things first. …
>
> And another way of achieving this is through showing a serious and sensible demeanour, and being always gentle, kindly, treating all alike, giving good example. And when conversing with people do not forget this prudent rule, well adapted to your situation, of speaking frankly and directly of the great principles of our religion, such as the love of Jesus Christ, faith, hope in God, charity towards one's neighbour, and so on. … it is as if you are scattering the seed here and there, and then waiting patiently for the Lord of the harvest to give the increase.[6]

Both Rinolfi and Signini were going to spend long years giving missions throughout the British Isles, so that these counsels from their Founder were pointing them along the correct path. Rosmini himself, notwithstanding his prodigious contribution to philosophy, had always shown great interest in pastoral work. The primacy of spiritual charity he illustrated through deep solicitude for what today we would call the faith development of parishioners. Indeed, he paid great attention, as the exhortations in his numerous letters to priests make clear, to the context in which people lived so as to encourage priests to ensure that their preaching fitted the needs of their congregation.

Rosmini was ahead of his time in this respect. The Vatican Council has instructed us to be sensitive to the 'signs of the times'.[7] Therefore, the difficulties which Protestants find with Catholicism is an aspect which should guide the way Catholic preachers shape their message.

In 1848 the English mission suffered a terrible blow. Luigi Gentili, the pioneer and their long-time leader, exhausted by his own missionary zeal, succumbed to the deadly typhus in Dublin while preaching in the very poorest part of the city. His companion Furlong was devastated, and it took him many months to recover not only from the shock of his companion's sudden death but also from the stress of constant missioning over a period of nearly four years.

Gentili's untimely death did not, however, mark the end of Rosminian preaching missions in Britain. In July 1849 Rinolfi was withdrawn from being a parish priest in Newport to become a full time missioner. It was in this ministry that he was to excel above all else.

NOTES

1   *The Catholic Magazine*, Vol. 1, Jan–June 1843, pp. 356–60.
2   Hirst, *op. cit., p. 52.*
3   *Hirst, op. cit., p. 45.*
4   *Rosminian archives.*
5   *The Ascetical Letters of Antonio Rosmini*, Vol. VI, no. 5.
6   *Ibid.*, Vol. VI, no. 4.
7   See Vatican II, *Gaudium et Spes*, 4.

5

THE FIRST MISSIONS

THE NINETEENTH CENTURY is often hailed as the high point of English literature, the age of Dickens, Thackeray, George Elliot, Jane Austen and the Brontës. But it was also a time of great oratory. The spoken word was the principal means of communication before telephones, telegrams, emails and television. For instance, the time of the Napoleonic wars was a golden age for parliamentary oratory: names like Burke, Fox and William Pitt, and later in the century, Robert Peel, Gladstone and Benjamin Disraeli, stand out.

Possibly the most celebrated of all these lay orators was the great anti–slavery warrior, William Wilberforce. Whenever he rose to speak in parliament, those present hung upon his every word. For more than twenty years he regaled parliamentarians with tales of the cruelty of the slave trade and the sheer iniquity of the institution of slavery. Vested interests stalled his earlier campaigns, but eventually his persuasive and relentless arguments prevailed over even the most hard-hearted, so that the 1807 Bill to abolish the slave trade passed almost unanimously in both Houses of Parliament.

It was also a time of great preachers. The weekly sermons of John Henry Newman in St Mary's University Church, Oxford, moulded the consciences of a whole generation of students, many of whom were destined to spend their lives as leaders in the Anglican Church. Earlier John Wesley had traversed the countryside on horseback preaching the Methodist revival. In the 1860s William Booth founded the Salvation Army, which promoted the ideals of social justice in the streets of the great industrial cities.

Angelo Rinolfi resembled Wilberforce in one signal characteristic: both were small of stature and insignificant in appear-
ance. Yet both had incomparable powers of persuasion. Through
the parish missions Rinolfi and his companions touched the
minds and hearts of countless Catholics in Britain and Ireland.
It would be no exaggeration to claim that during his years of
missioning Rinolfi brought about the conversion of thousands,
the return to faith and practice of tens of thousands, and the
strengthening of belief and fidelity of hundreds of thousands of
people. All this was achieved by word of mouth and without the
benefit of modern means of sound amplification.

We have referred above to the missions preached by Luigi
Gentili and Moses Furlong between 1845 and 1848. In that
final year they crossed to Ireland, where tragically Gentili
contracted typhus and died. The impression he had made there
during his short stay was such that his funeral in Dublin was
a triumph, and he was buried alongside the great Irish patriot
Daniel O'Connell in the Inner Circle of Glasnevin cemetery.
His memory continues to be honoured in Ireland to this day.

Though interrupted by Gentili's untimely death, a pattern
for the Rosminian missions had been established, and in 1849
Gentili's mantle fell onto Rinolfi's shoulders. Over the next
twenty-six years he gave more than 170 parish missions,
normally of two weeks' duration, but sometimes extended to
three and even four weeks. He travelled all over Britain: as far
north as Aberdeen in Scotland and even crossing the English
Channel to give a mission on the island of Guernsey. Like St
Paul's, his journeyings were constant and arduous.

He crossed the Irish Sea frequently, and eventually
preached more than fifty missions in Ireland. They are
described in a book entitled *Missions in Ireland*, published
anonymously in 1855 but undoubtedly written by Rinolfi
himself. Its style is simple and straightforward, and manifests
the complete grasp of the English language which Rinolfi

possessed. It describes vividly the problems faced in the west of Ireland following the devastating famine, and the attempts by evangelical Protestants to destroy Catholicism by a well-funded campaign of proselytism.

What Rinolfi does not describe in his book is the constant labour of travel which preaching missions over a wide area involved. By 1850 railway construction in England had established a network of over 10,000 miles of track. However, travelling considerable distances in the open carriages with wooden seats and belching smoke from the engines was anything but comfortable. Crossing the often turbulent Irish Sea aboard the primitive steam ferries was equally arduous. When Sir Robert Peel was Chief Secretary for Ireland in the second decade of the nineteenth century, he would regularly take nearly a week to travel from Dublin to London, and on one occasion the ferry from Dublin tossed and rolled in a storm for over twenty-four hours to get to Liverpool.

In all his writing Rinolfi never complains of the discomfort of travel nor about his frequent changes of bed and board. He took it all in his stride. He wrote cheerfully to his older brother in July 1855, casually mentioning the many retreats and missions he had given since he last wrote two years previously. As a postscript he says that 'if I have said nothing about my health, it is because it has ever remained good and excellent, as it still continues even now'. So, as well as being an exceptionally gifted preacher, he also rejoiced in a robust constitution which stood up well to all the rigours of travel and missioning.

In 1852, Rosmini appointed Rinolfi to be Vicar for the burgeoning English Province, which meant that he would be in charge during Pagani's frequent bouts of ill-health. The following year Rosmini, ever attentive to the English mission, wrote to Rinolfi directing him to exercise great care of the missioners, so that they would not work themselves into an early grave, as had happened to Gentili. He writes:

> I would like our missionaries to show great discretion
> so that they may not exhaust themselves all too soon
> from excessive work. I urgently ask you to care for
> their welfare and in particular those zealous workers,
> Furlong and Lockhart. To this end I would like the
> following two rules observed as far as possible: 1. That
> after three weeks work, or a month at most, there be
> eight or ten days rest before undertaking another
> mission; 2. That there be one day rest each week. I
> would add that the hours in the confessional be
> moderate, so that there be at least seven hours sleep.[1]

Wise words which Rinolfi himself would have taken to heart.

Gentili and Furlong were the forerunners and had established the pattern that was followed in most of the succeeding Rosminian missions. Rinolfi was assisted as chief missioner by various Rosminians. Furlong returned to the fray after his health had recovered. In the early years William Lockhart was often with him, and other Italians such as Bruno and Vilas. However, his most frequent companion was Fortunato Signini. In later years Signini was principally engaged in south Wales where he is acclaimed as the great Catholic pioneer, especially in Cardiff. Nevertheless he frequently took time off, so to speak, to be Rinolfi's mission companion and they made a powerful team. Signini himself was involved altogether in over eighty missions, a number only exceeded by Rinolfi himself.

All these men were great preachers. The Dominicans in London described Signini as 'another St Thomas Aquinas'.[2] Lockhart in later life was in perpetual demand in London and elsewhere as a public speaker, especially as a temperance campaigner. (In 1877 he was to give the oration at Rinolfi's own funeral.) Furlong had been a teacher of rhetoric, and his preaching was of such a quality that in Dublin young lawyers were known to attend his missions just to learn from his eloquent presentation.

ABERDEEN ○

GLASCOW

NEWCASTLE ○
DURHAM ○
STOCKTON-ON-TEES ○

YORK ○

MARKET WEIGHTON ○

BOLTON ○
STALYBRIDGE ○
MANCHESTER
LIVERPOOL ○

NOTTINGHAM ○
LOUGHBOROUGH ○
LEICESTER ○

BIRMINGHAM ○

RUGBY ○

SWANSEA
CARDIFF ○
NEWPORT
OXFORD ○

LONDON ○

BATH ○

SPETISBURY ○

Places of Rosminian interest and mission in Great Britain

It was Angelo Maria Rinolfi, however, who was undoubtedly the most accomplished. His zealous spirit, keen sense of purpose and love of language made him the master missioner. He had the gift of attracting and holding the attention of large numbers of people. His pronunciation of English was flawless, so that no one suspected that he was not a native English speaker. He had a powerful voice and could be heard by literally thousands of attendees, often out in the open because the churches could not always accommodate the numbers who wanted to hear him. It is significant that many who flocked to the missions probably as much out of curiosity as religious zeal, became hooked and returned if anything in greater numbers as the mission progressed.

At the beginning of his book about Rinolfi, Fr Joseph Hirst, testifies to his ability as a preacher:

> If there are many who remember Fr Rinolfi as a short-statured, dark-complexioned, and in countenance somewhat ill-favoured foreigner, it may have been to them at times a matter of some wonderment how so insignificant a person, possessed of seemingly such great natural disadvantages, should have accomplished so much.

He then goes on to describe his remarkable talent as a speaker:

> as a preacher he would lift up his voice in the pulpit and forthwith, as if by some instantaneous and magnetic influence, take possession of his auditory [audience], or at other times seem to animate as it were a whole platform by his rapid movement to and fro and with his determined look, flashing eye and stirring gesture, hold a vast congregation spellbound by his eloquence.[3]

This biography was written only a few years after Rinolfi's death, and the author had had personal experience of his subject, as well as full access to other Rosminians who had known Rinolfi well.

This somewhat flamboyant style of declaiming from the pulpit was common enough in Victorian times, probably more so in Italy. There is an entertaining account of such preaching in Axel Munthe's famous book *The Story of San Michele*. The occasion was the feast-day of Sant'Antonio, patron of Anacapri, where Munthe was living at that time. He was present at the celebration and describes the sermon (the time would have been about 1900):

> At 11 the sermon was given from the pulpit in commemoration of Sant'Antonio and his miracles, each miracle illustrated and made visible by a gesture appropriate to the occasion. Now the orator would raise his hands in ecstasy to the saints in heaven, now he would point his index finger to the floor to locate the underground dwellings of the damned.
>
> Now he would fall on his knees in silent prayers to Sant'Antonio suddenly to spring to his feet on the point of precipitating himself from the pulpit to smite down an invisible scoffer with a blow of his fist. Now he would bow his head in rapturous silence to listen to the happy chants of the angels, now, pale with terror, he would put his hands to his ears so as not to hear the grinding of the teeth of *Il Demonio* and the cries of the sinners in their cauldrons. At last, steaming with perspiration and prostrated by the sobs and maledictions, at a temperature of 105 Fahrenheit, he would sink down on the floor of the pulpit with a terrible curse on the Protestants.[4]

Munthe's description is something of a caricature. Rinolfi would never have had to encounter a temperature of 105 degrees Fahrenheit in Britain or Ireland, and he was certainly too charitable to curse Protestants; nor perhaps would all his sermons have been quite on the scale of the one described for that patronal feast day. But it is as well to realise that the Italians of that era knew how to put on a spectacular performance.

After all, in a world without cinema or TV, the mission would have been the best show in town, and an eloquent preacher like Rinolfi would, and did, draw in the crowds. The sermons were set in the frame of liturgies of a quality and interest which the normal English or Irish parish would never have experienced before. The pattern of singing, processions, devotions to Mary and the saints, especially the Forty Hours' Devotion before the Blessed Sacrament exposed, and the concluding candle-lit liturgy for the renewal of baptismal promises: all these were new experiences to the people.

The missions also included many opportunities to receive the sacraments. Hundreds went to confession, it being the custom to bring in priests from surrounding parishes to help. Many more received communion—often more than once, and that in an age when such frequency was very rare. Children and adult converts were baptised. It was common for the local bishop to attend and give confirmation to those who had not already received that sacrament.

As a consequence of attending these missions, very many Catholics returned to a more regular practice of their faith, those who were lax or who had apostatised were reconciled, and others, even atheists, were converted to Catholicism. There is no doubt that the introduction of parish missions into England by the Rosminians—and soon to be augmented by Redemptorists, Passionists and Jesuits—was a major factor in the restoration of the Catholic faith in Britain and its powerful renewal in Ireland.

Rinolfi was scrupulous in making notes, listing and describing these early missions. In his diaries the same central themes of wide and growing participation keep recurring: he speaks of the high attendances which tended to increase as the mission proceeded. This was just as true for smaller country parishes as for the cities. In the country people were often prepared to walk for miles in order to be present. He speaks of 'thousands' attending, although it is difficult to imagine how these numbers could be counted. They were simply estimates.

One who accompanied him said this:

> Fr Rinolfi was gifted with a natural eloquence with which he riveted the attention of his hearers. I have sat listening to him speaking for two hours without being wearied. ... His sermons on the Blessed Sacrament—an exposition of the sixth chapter of St John—on the Blessed Virgin Mary and on the holy sacrament of Penance, were so closely reasoned as to be the most complete I ever heard on these subjects.[5]

There was some hostility to the missions from Protestants, but this was only a serious problem in Ireland with the Orangemen in the north and the activity of the so-called 'Proselytisers' in the west. Indeed, in many places the missions drew interest and support from beyond the Catholic community. In one place in the north of England for example, a Methodist minister invited Rinolfi to preach a series of sermons in his own chapel after the mission was over, but regrettably Rinolfi was unable to oblige.

Much has been said of the interest in Rinolfi's missions shown by the press, especially *The Tablet* and local papers in England and Ireland. Here is what the *Catholic Standard* in Liverpool reported on the mission in St Peter's Chapel, Seel Street in December 1850:

> His sermon on the Day of Judgment was a most extraordinary piece of pulpit oratory. So vividly did he present it that the people were moved to tears. The fervid eloquence from this noble preacher's lips struck not only the ear but the heart ... he would inspire with life every subject he touched on.
>
> On Sunday night the same priest delivered another of those discourses which really bewilders the mind whilst it enchants the soul. The subject was Baptism, and Fr

Rinolfi gave an excellent and lucid exposition of the sacrament and its obligations.[6]

The paper also describes the final evening service for renewal of baptismal promises, when 3,000 candles were lit and the altar was magnificently illuminated.

The distinctiveness of the style of Rosminian missions reflects the doctrine of universal charity, foundational to Antonio Rosmini's spiritual teaching. Rosmini speaks of a threefold division of charity. By charity he means the Christian sense of the term as the highest form of love exemplified by God's love for humanity, always selfless, benevolent and applied equally to all.

The three components comprise: *Temporal charity* which is 'hands on', practical and ethical, even political; *Spiritual charity* which is the sphere of good liturgy, of prayer and devotional practice; *Intellectual charity*—a special mark of Rosminian teaching—which consists of the necessary basis of theology; the theologian seeks God's truth and love, and the catechist guides others to God's love and truth, as a service of love to them. These three are united in universal charity. The *spiritual* connects us directly with God; the *intellectual* discovers who God is; the *temporal* is the practical outcome. Embodied in the person, universal charity when exercised becomes an act of love for the other, and so we see in Rinolfi, and indeed all the missioners, not just a sense of duty but a deep care for those to whom they ministered.

Temporal charity—perhaps the key to attracting so many to attend the missions—leads the missioner to discover and hold present any social or ethical problems among parishioners: are there divisions to be healed? Is alcoholism or severe poverty an issue? What are the pressing local social challenges? *Spiritual charity* directs the liturgical life of the mission: its emphasis is on the sacraments; daily Eucharist; teaching on prayer; praying contemplatively. *Intellectual charity* is expressed by lectures on the moral and ethical teachings of the Church, delivered with the hope of transforming the lives of the participants.

There was special emphasis on sacramental theology. The call to repent and change one's life demands careful preparation and opportunity in the sacrament of Penance. The process continues on into Eucharist, even received daily. And if new people, adults and children, are to be brought into the Church, this will involve having public services of baptism and confirmation.

Unfortunately, we have no copies of the actual text of Rinolfi's sermons. But the outlines that have been found in his papers and diaries indicate that he was a traditionalist rather than an innovator. What the people needed was a grounding in the basics, and that is what they got. Rinolfi's job was to pass on the teachings of the Church, and to introduce the people to Scripture and the wisdom and spirituality of the ages past in a way that engaged their temporal, spiritual and doctrinal needs.

Here are two examples of his early missions in England. Bolton is a typical manufacturing town in Lancashire. The congregation would have been largely working class northerners, and there would have been a number of recent Irish immigrants. The mission took place in October 1851 and Rinolfi's companion was William Lockhart. The quotation below comes from Rinolfi's diary.

> This is the second time we preached a mission here. We found several people from the last mission, who have persevered faithfully in a good life. One man who then, for the first time in his life (of 40 years), had come to Confession, came to me again and assured me that he had never missed since. But many more have fallen away to the great grief of their pastors.

> This mission was continued for three weeks and except for the first two or three days, the chapel was filled to suffocation every night. Hundreds of stray sheep have

again been reclaimed. May it be forever! Several Protestants, perhaps 20, have been received into the Church and prepared for Communion and Confession. Nearly 1000 were confirmed on the last Sunday by the Bishop of Salford.

A few weeks later the mission team was in the much larger city of Liverpool at St Anne's parish, Edge Hill (16–30 November).

I began the mission alone, Fr Lockhart having gone from Bolton to Aberford and York and engaged to preach at Clifton … He arrived on Monday 17. The mission was well attended and succeeded better than we could have expected. The church was never so well filled before, since its erection. It is away from the bulk of the Catholic population and extremely cold, and the pastor is not well liked since he is not much of a preacher …

Many Catholics who were out of the Church or had made bad confessions or who were living unmarried made their peace with God. A whole family of eight or ten persons were out of the Church, the children being sent to Protestant schools in imminent danger of losing their faith, were brought back to their duties and the children sent to a Catholic school …

In the various places where we have preached missions, but especially in the large towns, we have often seen how terribly persecuted as regards their religion are poor Catholic servants. Everything is done by their masters to prevent them practising their religion …

Rinolfi also refers to some interesting liturgical features for Lent he had initiated:

Here for the first time in public missions we introduced the service on the seven blood sheddings of Our Blessed Lord and on the seven words from the Cross, on the two Fridays of the mission: they seemed to make a deep impression. The crucifix was illuminated by a circle of candles: there was a short sermon followed by prayers and a verse from the *Stabat Mater* sung by the choir after each blood shedding, which made the service both interesting and impressive …

At the same time the mission was going on, the Devil managed to bring to Liverpool an unfortunate Italian priest named Gavarini, who, on some evenings at the same time we were preaching at St Anne's, was declaiming against the Pope and the Church, addressing a group of some 500 English fanatics who understood scarcely a word of what he said. They were quite sure that it was all right and beautiful because it was against the Church. Poor silly John Bull—how gullible thou art!

However, this sort of active opposition was rare in the English missions.

In November 1852 he crossed the Irish Sea again and gave his first mission in Galway, followed in December by another at St Audeon's parish in Dublin. After that, Ireland for a time became the main scene of his missioning, especially in the west where the effects of the recent potato famine were devastating. Between July 1855 and July 1857 Rinolfi crossed to Ireland and back four times, as well as travelling to London twice, and also to Edinburgh and Dundee. The Irish missions will be fully described in a following chapter.

The majority of the missions in England were in the north because that is where most of the Catholic population lived. As a missioner Rinolfi was echoing the restless meanderings of St Paul, but preaching to many more people, without, however, the danger of being robbed or thrown into prison.

In 1855 Rinolfi was appointed Provincial of the English Province. This did not mean the cessation of his missions, but he now had the added responsibilities of regularly visiting the parishes in south Wales as well as the industrial schools run by the Rosminians at Market Weighton in Yorkshire, at Upton in County Cork in the south of Ireland, and at Sainghin in the north of France.

For twenty years he combined the duties of being Provincial Superior while continuing to preach at retreats and missions. He made Rugby in central England his residence, although he was often away as much as he was at home. And even in Rugby he sometimes added further roles, acting for a time as novice master or parish priest. He was a man of ceaseless and selfless activity for God. For most of his life he was blessed with very good health, otherwise none of this would have been possible in the conditions of the time.

NOTES

1   *The Ascetical Letters of Antonio Rosmini,* Vol. VIII, no. 44.
2   Hill, J. M., *The Rosminian Mission,* p. 22.
3   Hirst, *op. cit.,* p. 1.
4   A. Munthe, *The Story of San Michele* (London: John Murray, 1929), p. 468.
5   *Hirst, op.cit., p. 65.*
6   *Catholic Standard, 21 December, 1850,* p. 7.

6

MISSIONS IN IRELAND

A^{T THE TIME} when Rinolfi began his career as a full-time missioner, the situation in England was being overshadowed by the terrible disaster occurring across the Irish Sea. The Irish potato famine was the most serious single disaster in Europe of the nineteenth century in terms of human misery and loss of life. The famine started when the potato blight appeared suddenly across Europe in 1845. But the human tragedy was greatest in the west of Ireland where potatoes were the staple diet.

The Irish Nationalist John Mitchell summed up the disaster thus: 'The Almighty, indeed, sent the potato blight, but the English created the famine'. It happened after centuries of neglect and oppression on the part of successive British governments, and the Prime Minister, Sir Robert Peel, was sufficiently concerned that in 1843 he appointed a Royal Commission to assess the social situation in Ireland. The Commission reported early in 1845, and its findings were devastating.

'Ireland is a conquered country and the Irish peasant is a dispossessed man, his landlord an alien conqueror'. The root cause of Irish misery and poverty, it stated, was the prevailing bad relationship between landlord and tenant. The landlords were for the most part absentees and 'regarded the soil of Ireland merely as a source from which to extract as much money as possible'. Sadly, the report, and the remedial measures proposed by Peel came too late. Before the government knew what was happening the famine struck with overwhelming effect.

Peel at once bought maize at a value of £100,000 sterling from America and imported it into the famine-stricken areas.

The following year he abolished the Corn Laws which for decades had protected English agriculture from foreign competition, with the immediate effect of lowering the price of bread all over Britain and Ireland. Unfortunately, Peel's government was driven from power, and the succeeding Liberal administration simply ignored the tragedy which was unfolding across the Irish Sea. The potato crop failed successively each year until there was some recovery in 1850. By that time a million Irish people had died of starvation and disease, and another million had fled the country.

Most of the refugees sought to escape to the United States, the land of promise, but only some could afford the cost of the Atlantic sea voyage. Thousands instead settled in England, Scotland and Wales, largely unwelcome but at least still alive. They brought with them typhus—the so-called famine fever—which created further problems and animosity towards the new migrants. Mostly they were at least nominal Catholics and they presented a huge challenge to the Church in Britain. Among the most effective responses to this influx were the parish missions, so the Rosminians soon became heavily involved.[1] The missions usually attracted many of the new immigrants, giving them some measure of consolation in their faith and helping to integrate them into existing parishes.

The first missions in Ireland itself had been delivered in Dublin by Fathers Luigi Gentili and Moses Furlong. The two missioners arrived after three years of well-supported missions in England and Wales, and although there had been eloquent appeals for them to go to Ireland, it was not until April 1848 that they were finally able to cross the Irish Sea to Dublin.

They found the city in a state of turmoil because of threats of insurrection. Anti-English feeling, which had been simmering for many years, was intensified by the effects of the famine. After the death of the famous Irish patriot, Daniel O'Connell, who had always counselled only peaceful protest against the iniquities of

British rule, the baton was taken up by the so-called *Young Ireland* movement, led by William Smith O'Brien: this organisation promoted confrontation and armed rebellion. Ten thousand troops were mobilised in the city to counter these threats. This tense atmosphere did not bode well for the parish missions.

However, once the preaching began—in the very large but yet to be completed church of St Audeon in High Street—the religious zeal aroused in the crowds attending had a calming effect. This first mission was followed by a second, month-long mission in the parish of Rathmines. Great crowds flocked to hear the two preachers, and the confessionals were besieged well into the night. Nothing like this had ever been seen before.

After Rathmines, they accepted a third mission in the Augustinian chapel of St John's, in Thomas Street, a very poor area of the city where typhus was widespread. The missioners were strongly advised not to go there, but Gentili was adamant: 'Are there not souls to save in the slums as much as in the more favoured areas?' he asked.

The pressure of this third mission was intense. Gentili wrote:

> The crowd is so great that we just do not know where to turn. Unfortunately, the local priests are so busy they cannot help us in the labours of the confessional: the weight therefore falls entirely on us, so that with great effort we succeed in gathering only one-third of the fruit we could gather if other labourers could come to our help.

One can detect a cry from the heart in these words. Indeed, a few days into the mission Gentili suddenly fell ill while hearing confessions, and had to retire to bed. He was physically exhausted and therefore a prey to infection. His health rapidly deteriorated, and on 26 September he succumbed to the deadly disease of typhus. His death caused a sensation in the city: crowds flocked to honour his body, and, as has been mentioned, he was buried at Glasnevin cemetery close to the tomb of Daniel O'Connell.

Rinolfi's first missions in Ireland

Gentili's untimely death end put an end to the Rosminians' public missioning for several months. Furlong too was exhausted by the pressure of the previous three years, and it took him a long time to recover from that and from the shock of Gentili's death. Public missions resumed the following year in 1849 when Angelo Maria Rinolfi was appointed to this task on a permanent basis. This was to be his principal pastoral ministry for the rest of his life.

We are fortunate to have Rinolfi's own published account of the Irish missions—*Missions in Ireland*—but he modestly conceals his authorship with the by-line 'One of the Missioners'. The reader may judge how completely he had equipped himself to write fluently and interestingly in English. He sometimes apologises for of his lack of fluency in Irish, and in the west of Ireland he often needed the assistance of a translator.

These missions were a huge achievement, but it is significant that when he was engaged full-time he never preached more than twelve missions in a year. In other words he accepted Rosmini's words of fraternal advice and took the occasional regular break. By comparison, in the three years of Gentili's missionary apostolate he and Furlong had given over fifty-five missions. Such a regime was simply beyond human strength.

Rinolfi's first visit to Ireland was to Dublin in May 1850. Furlong was booked to accompany him but was still unwell, so Rinolfi ventured forth on his own. The mission was in the parish of St Nicholas Without. He was duly impressed, and noted 'the pious simplicity, and the joyful open countenances of the poor, in the midst of their poverty and privations, the humility and devotion of the higher classes, and the attachment of all to their religion'.

He preached two or three times a day to a packed church with none of the helpful sound systems available today. It was little wonder that once or twice he lost his voice and had to take a break. By and large, however, his constitution was robust enough to withstand the rigours of these highly pressured missions.

Entering into the various Catholic churches and chapels, he saw hundreds of Catholics at all hours every day in the week, either attending to the Holy Sacrifice of the Mass, filling the Communion rails, surrounding the confessionals, humbly and devoutly adoring their hidden God, or going piously through the stations of the cross. He felt that he was in a Catholic city again after several years spent in the cold Protestant atmosphere of England.[2]

The parish of St Nicholas Without was one of the biggest and poorest in the city, but the church in Francis Street, St Nicholas of Myra, was large and handsome and capable of holding over 3000 people. Following this first mission when Rinolfi was on his own, he was invited to another parish, St Andrew's, one of the wealthiest in Dublin with a very grand church in Westland Row. Rinolfi describes it as 'the largest church in Dublin, and may contain from six to seven thousand persons'. So, during this introductory time in Ireland, Rinolfi experienced both the poor and the well-to-do, although the faith-filled reception and the crowds were much the same in both locations.

The first mission was held in the month of May, and Rinolfi preached an interesting homily on chapter twelve of the book of Revelation. The way he interpreted the symbolism of Revelation would probably raise eyebrows among modern Scripture scholars. Nevertheless he was successful in arousing the devotion of the people in the month dedicated to Mary.

Another theme he used at St Andrew's was that of pilgrimage: the pilgrim encounters both consolation and the desolation of the Cross on his journey, and so the faithful soul must be prepared to seek the 'narrow way which leads to eternal life'. Rinolfi was subtly suggesting to his audience that wealth and prosperity are not the important goals to seek for in life, but in the Providence of God we must always be prepared for trials and deprivations too, which in time will strengthen us. It is in this way that the faithful Christian participates in carrying the Cross of Christ.

This brief first sojourn in Dublin was for Rinolfi an overture for what was to be one of the principal fields of his future apostolate. Following the devastating effects in the west of Ireland of the potato famine of 1845–8, it was to those counties bordering the Atlantic Ocean that he returned many times. There he saw the greatest need, and it became his top priority.

———•—•—•———

Rinolfi came back to Ireland the following year, 1851, this time with Lockhart, and together they preached missions right across the country. Lockhart was one of the earliest English Rosminians, and appears to have had a special sympathy towards and affection for the Irish people.

He had been a disciple of John Henry Newman at Oxford and followed him to Littlemore, the retreat outside the city where Newman and his close followers formed a semi-monastic community. After a year—and to Newman's horror—Lockhart decided to go to Loughborough where Gentili was parish priest and do a retreat with him. This was a mind-blowing experience for the young man: he decided to become a Catholic at once and applied to join the Rosminians. For a time Newman strongly disapproved of Lockhart's hasty action, but two years later, in 1845, Newman himself followed him into the Catholic Church, and the two friends became reconciled.

After ordination to the priesthood, Lockhart joined the missioning team and was often Rinolfi's companion. Their first joint mission, in February-March 1851, was at St Audeon's Church, in High Street, Dublin. Then they went north, and in April gave the very first ever mission in Belfast.

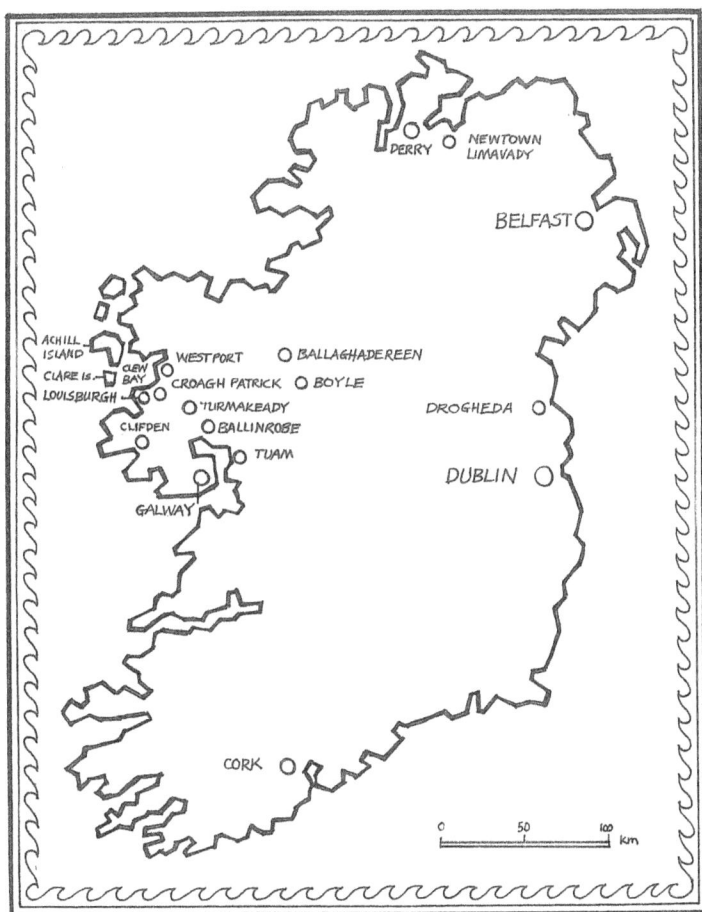

Places of Rosminian interest and mission in Ireland

The town of Belfast was growing rapidly as a result of the creation of the linen industry, and it became known as the 'Manchester' of Ireland. The new factories attracted an influx of workers, many of whom were Catholic. This mission took place at a large, modern church, St Malachy's, but such was the size of the crowds who came, they soon had to employ a second church, St Patrick's in Donegal Street, with one missioner in each venue. The mission took place during Holy

Week and over Easter, and during the final week both churches were packed every day.

Altogether, more than 10,000 people received the Eucharist, and on the final night both churches were filled to overflowing for a candle service and the renewal of Baptismal vows. The next day the two missioners made their way to the docks to board the ferry back to Liverpool. To their amazement they were accompanied by a great crowd of people, who assembled on the quay and knelt for a final blessing after the priests had gone on board ship.

One of the themes that Rinolfi would always emphasise was the need for repentance as a preparation for the Sacrament of Reconciliation. He would sometimes warn the people not to be complacent: they might have to face a sudden fatal accident or unexpected mortal illness, so they should always be prepared. Thus the Sacrament of Reconciliation became an integral part of every mission.

However, he also reassured them with the promise that the Church would always strive to prepare people well. Indeed, it is apparent that Rinolfi believed the sacraments should be offered liberally as an expression of the Church's merciful heart. Here Rinolfi foreshadows a development in the Church's teaching on the sacraments—that they are a necessary medicine rather than a prize for good behaviour.

Rinolfi writes: 'there is no place, ever so poor or wretched, or infected with the most contagious disease, where a poor sinner lies, into which the priest of God will not venture, at the imminent danger of his own life, to afford a chance of salvation to the most abandoned of sinners'.[3]

Another characteristic of the Rosminian mission that Rinolfi emphasised was the need for frequent communion:

> as a fruit of their Mission among them, the faithful should *frequently* approach the Holy Communion for the remainder of their lives … they would still exhort

them to approach as frequently as possible the great
supper, some, every week, and even several times in
the week; others, every fortnight; others, again, every
month; all, more than once a year.[4]

It is significant that the Rosminian missioners should stress
this regularity of practice, which we take for granted, at a time
when people approached the table of the Lord only rarely, and
indeed it was sixty years before Pope Pius X made the habit
of frequent communion a norm in the Church.

Lockhart personally was always a source of fascination to the
people because he was a convert from Anglicanism: whenever
he spoke of his own conversion a murmur of joy and gratitude
would spontaneously rise up from the congregation. He would
sometimes quote from Anglican prayer books such as the *Book
of Common Prayer* which spoke of the need for absolution of sins
and confession. However, his personal experience had been that
the Anglican Church had preached the necessity of confession
in theory but rejected it in practice. Therefore he had sought out
the Catholic Church, which not only taught the necessity of
confession but actually provided the sacrament.

A local Protestant paper gave the mission a glowing report.

> The ardent eloquence, by which the daily discourses
> of both the gentlemen are distinguished, is of a
> character so attractive that a great many, not Roman
> Catholics, attend in St. Malachy's Chapel, at the
> specified hours, for the purpose of hearing them. Each
> morning, after an early Mass, one of the preachers
> addresses the people; and, each evening, both gentle-
> men deliver discourses. These are directed with a view
> to the full inculcation of the broad principles of charity
> and moral rectitude; but as the special object of the
> Mission is to give an opportunity to the Roman
> Catholics to perform one of the sacraments of that
> Church—the sacrament of penance—the exhortations
> of the clergy are directed in a special manner to an

explanation of the conditions laid down by the Church
as necessary for the proper reception of the sacrament.
The mere matter of preaching is a very subordinate
portion of the duties of the Missioners. It is in the
confessionals their labours are onerous,—indeed,
remarkably severe.[5]

Not all the newspapers painted such a favourable and understanding picture of the mission, for the Orange lodges
controlled much of the local press: these were strident in their
objections and mockery of this 'papistry'. However, both here
and elsewhere many Protestants were not merely interested
but supportive of the evident moral and religious benefits the
missions brought.

Rinolfi's missions were not confined to the major cities. In
October 1853, for instance, he was invited to give a mission at
St Peter's church in Drogheda, an ancient town some forty miles
north of Dublin. It is famous in history for the siege and
massacre perpetrated against the Catholics by Oliver Cromwell
in 1649, and also for the nearby battle of the Boyne in 1690
when William of Orange defeated the Catholic army of King
James II.

The local Drogheda paper wrote enthusiastically of the
mission:

> On Sunday last, the Rev. Fathers. Rinolfi and Vilas, of
> the Order of Charity, commenced their pious labours
> in St. Peter's Catholic Church. The Mission was
> opened by a powerful sermon from the first named
> Father, and certainly the fame that preceded the gifted
> preacher was more than fully sustained. Clear, logical,
> and impressive in style, he descanted on the moral and
> eternal truths of Christianity, and enforced the obliga-
> tions of repentance in a manner to rivet the hearts of
> all, and to bring conviction on the most hardened.

Never before, in the memory of any man living in this town, were the grand influences of religion brought so powerfully to bear upon the minds and hearts of the faithful. We know not what most to admire in this manifestation of God's merciful designs; whether we dwell on the powerful, practical, and instructive oratory of Father Rinolfi and his companion, or the beauty and grandeur of the ceremonies of the Church, or the unusual crowds of penitents flocking from all quarters to the tribunal of confession, or the vast multitude daily approaching the table of the Lord—we must acknowledge that great blessings have been poured down upon the people of Drogheda. ...

Many benefits in the spiritual order have been granted to Drogheda; the town has been highly favoured on many occasions, and many brilliant lights have shone here from time to time; but this Mission has done more good than can be estimated, more than could have been expected by the most sanguine. Sinners, the most abandoned, have been reclaimed; sinners, whose habits would have marked them out as reprobates, have come, as at the preaching of John the Baptist, confessing their sins, and renouncing their ways. About 12,000 people went to confession, and received the Holy Eucharist during the short space of three weeks.[6]

Drogheda was primarily a Catholic town, so one might expect a welcoming tone in the local press. But in other towns, particularly where the Orange influence was strong, this was not always the case. One such town with a strong Orange presence was Newtown Limavady, in the north west some twelve miles from Derry, which Rinolfi visited in August 1854. Only a minority of the population of the town would have been Catholics.

Nevertheless, the mission itself was a success, and a letter to *The Tablet* (signed J. M. C.) paid tribute to the excellence of the preaching:

> By a series of truly eloquent sermons, these zealous Fathers demonstrated that the primary end of man's creation was to serve and love God, and that whatever was conducive to the attainment of that end, must be done at any cost. They next proceeded to show that sin alone deprives man of his lofty destiny, and to point out the enormity of sin from the severe punishment with which a God, whose most conspicuous attribute is mercy, visited it in the apostate Angels.
>
> The Very Reverend Father Rinolfi, with that simplicity and that close reasoning which characterise all his discourses, proved the folly of man in sinning for sake of pleasures and advantages arising from it even if there was nothing to be apprehended beyond the grave; but what an excess of folly is man guilty of by sin, when he considers the judgment?[7]

The attendance was very good and people came from far and wide to be present for the sessions over a period of two weeks. Indeed so many arrived for the final liturgy that the church was far too small to contain the concourse of over 20,000 people, so a platform was erected in a local field (lent for the occasion by a sympathetic owner) for the candle ceremony and renewal of baptismal vows.

> The Mission was closed by imparting to all who attended it, whether absent or present, His Holiness's benediction blessing, thanking God for His protection and assistance, and offering up a fervent prayer for all dissenting neighbours ... one of the local clergy ... called upon the people to give three cheers for the Pope, for their Bishop, for the Missioners, and for the owner of the field. We need not say with what readiness, energy, and force, the call was responded to by the

enthusiastic Catholics, at the termination of such a glorious work as they had witnessed, done by the right hand of God in their midst.

However, this peaceful scene was then suddenly interrupted by an infuriated mob of Orangemen, and ugly and violent scenes followed.

> Down they rushed like wolves on the fold, and yelling like furies, some armed with bludgeons, others with swords and tongs, and some with hidden, more deadly, weapons. When they reached the Catholics, the latter were retiring peacefully, as became people retiring from such a solemn and sacred ceremony; they were set upon and beaten most savagely—some fled, some were driven to the church gate.

> At this period Fr Rinolfi … was proceeding from the field to the Parish Priest's house, when hearing of the attack made by the Orange mob upon the Catholics, he hastened to the spot, not far from the church, on the high-road, in the hope of preventing any serious injury, and found himself in the midst of men, who truly looked like demons.

> He addressed one of them boldly; and this man seemed as if he had become powerless and unable to wield his mortal weapon, and drew back begging pardon; but another man, in the meantime, gave the Father a blow on the back of the head with a club or an iron bar, and had not the Father immediately been surrounded by Catholics and rescued from their hands, the scoundrels would have taken his life.

> Several persons suffered very severe injuries on the skull and other parts; a poor young woman, in partic-ular, struck by a very large stone on the face, fell down senseless, and covered with blood was carried away as dead, though she afterwards recovered. If no more harm to life or limb was done, it is clearly to be

attributed to the patience and Christian forbearance of the poor innocent Catholics, and to the efforts made by the Missioners and clergy to preserve peace. ...

In the meantime the constabulary was called out, but their efforts to quell the riot did not much restrain the Protestant party. After the ferocious band had satisfied themselves against the persons of Catholics, and quiet had been in some degree restored, they proceeded to wreck and destroy all the Catholic houses in Newtown Limavady; not a single window in the houses occupied by the Catholics in the town, was spared—except one—they did not leave even a parcel of miserable huts unmolested, whose poverty and insignificance should have shielded them from their ferocity; and after wreaking their vengeance on the houses, those furies turned their minds to the Catholic church, and agreed to demolish it.

They procured for this purpose, a large quantity of gunpowder, and two pieces of cannon, generally used for salutes on the 12th of July, and on other such occasions; but, fortunately, some of their guides saw the folly of this and prevented it, and the Orangemen concluded the night with a general jubilee over the extermination of Popery in Newtown Limavady.[8]

This scandal was not wholly ignored by the authorities, and several of the perpetrators were sent for trial.

These horrible events took place in 1855, the year that Antonio Rosmini died, and Rinolfi was due to attend the election of his successor as General of the Rosminians. But he was unable to go since he was a principal witness at the trial of the Orange vandals. In the event the charges were dismissed by the magistrate on the grounds that the accused had indicated remorse for what they had done. So they got off scot-free! Such was the justice that the Catholics were accustomed to receive in those parts of Ireland where the Orange influence was powerful. However, this degree of hostility was rare.

Missions in the West of Ireland

Between 1850 and 1855, when Rinolfi became the English Provincial, he preached over twenty parish missions in the west of Ireland, in the areas where the effects of the famine had been greatest. It was precisely for this reason and the pressing needs of the surviving population that the Rosminians made this region a priority for their missioning endeavours. The local bishops issued the invitations, so the missioners came back at regular intervals, especially to the dioceses of Galway, Tuam and Achonry.

When they first arrived in Galway in November 1852, what they found horrified them. Rinolfi describes the initial impact:

> Language can scarcely describe the impression made on them by the vestiges, which, on their way from Dublin to Galway met their eyes in every direction, of the dreadful havoc made, of late years, in that part of the country, partly by the last famine, and partly by English misrule, and the unfeeling conduct of land-lords. Thousands swept away by the famine, and thousands, again, obliged to look for a morsel of bread in foreign countries, seemed to have left the land almost desolate.
>
> The humble huts in which they lived have, in many cases, been razed to the ground, while the gables of others seem to have been left standing, by a just and adorable Providence, only as monuments of the fearful sufferings undergone by their former inhabitants. And what suggested itself to their minds during their journey was fully confirmed to them during their sojourn in the town of Galway.

They were informed that persons were not infrequently, in the years of famine, seen walking, or rather tottering like ghosts, through the streets and lanes of the city, and then dropping down dead, and often lying dead by hedges and ditches. Several of these poor creatures chose to die, rather than take by violence or by fraud any article of food, as they thought, unjustly from others.

Two parishes in the neighbourhood of Galway, which, before the famine, were very flourishing and counted about 12,000 inhabitants each, have been reduced, by death and emigration, to about 4,000 each.[9]

This dreadful depopulation was by no means confined to Galway. It occurred right through the centre of Ireland as well, but it was especially evident on the west coast, where dependence on the potato as the staple diet had been greatest. For instance, in the parish of Turmakeady and Partree, which the missioners came to in April 1853, they found grave evidence of depopulation and dire poverty.

Both morning and evening, and indeed all the day long, hundreds were to be seen in the chapel or approaching the Sacraments. The population is not now one-third of what it was before the famine; the people are scattered all over that locality, and the villages, of which the parish is composed, are but a few thatched hovels, the poorest that can be imagined.

The parish extends over twelve miles, and still from every part the poor people came to the Mission, some of them having to walk some miles by night over mountain paths dangerous even by day. The havoc produced by the famine in this part of the country was perfectly awful and incredible. ...

The Parish Priest pointed out to the Missioners a spot where stood during the famine a small cottage, in which a mother with her son and daughter had been found dead, the daughter having her teeth in the flesh of the arm of her poor mother. The patience and resignation with which all those poor creatures had endured the pangs of hunger, and the horrors of death, the constancy with which they clung to their religion in those calamitous times, as we were assured everywhere, must have contributed much to prepare them for heaven.[10]

Rinolfi and his companions were horrified by the poverty and destitution of so many of the inhabitants in these remote areas of Ireland, but since they themselves were so far away from their base in Rugby, they were not in a position to do much to alleviate the distress. However, they were able to observe the work of the religious Orders which had come to the west, presumably at the invitation of the bishops. There were Franciscans on Achill Ireland and the Presentation Sisters and the Sisters of Mercy in various other parishes, who deliberately came to the places where the need was greatest to serve the people and educate their children. The Rosminian preachers simply provided the spiritual background for the hands-on work of these dedicated Religious.

What is astonishing is the faithfulness with which the local people embraced the opportunities given to them by the missions. The numbers who flocked to the little churches were proportionately just as great as in Dublin and the towns to the east. Even when the weather was wet and stormy, as it frequently is on the west coast, they still arrived in their hundreds and their thousands.

Rinolfi comments on this aspect during the mission in January 1853 at Clifden, a coastal town in Connemara.

> The Mission lasted a fortnight; the weather was more or less the same throughout, rainy and stormy in the extreme, the roads dirty and dangerous, the people

scattered all over that mountainous country. And still, as the Mission was proceeding, the faith and devotion of the people became every day more striking and intense. The chapel was full from morning till late in the evening, at night it was crammed to suffocation.

People flocked in from all parts of Connemara; and many of them, after having spent the whole day in attending to the sermons and the other devotions, and in endeavouring to get to confession (though often disappointed), had to walk, after the evening sermon, which was not over before nine o'clock, eight and ten miles, through rain and wind, in the darkness of the night.

On the second Sunday of the Mission, the crowd was so great that all the windows of the chapel had to be taken out, in order that the people within might be able to breathe, and those without hear the sermons.[11]

Naturally enough Rinolfi never suggests that it was the quality of the preaching which drew so many to the missions in the first place and persuaded them to persevere to the end. But it is revealing to read what a newspaper in Galway city had to say about Lockhart and Rinolfi:

Within our own memory we have never witnessed any scene like that which the several chapels of this town, in which the Missionaries preached, presented, night after night, since their arrival in Galway. Had it occurred once or twice, or thrice, it might, perhaps, be supposed that many who attended these discourses were attracted by novelty, or some other frivolous cause. But when each successive evening beheld a concourse larger than the previous one, and saw every available spot in which the speaker's words were audible crowded even to suffocation, and when the anxiety to be present was as great on the last night as upon the first or any subsequent one, it is evident that a circumstance so unusual must have its origin in a far higher motive then idle curiosity.

The truth is, that the very first sermons preached by Fathers Rinolfi and Lockhart created a deep and permanent impression upon all who heard them, and their splendid and persuasive eloquence, combined with their masterly method of treating the all-important subjects which they handled, awakened feelings long dormant, and touched a chord silent perhaps for many years in many a heart, but which now responded to the solemn and earnest appeals which fell from lips touched with the fire of ardent charity and exalted devotion.[12]

During these missions the missioners introduced devotions such as the Forty Hours' adoration, which the people were unfamiliar with, and these had a profound impact. During the mission at Boyle in May 1853 this devotion was held following the feast of Corpus Christi. Some of the priests who were present reported:

The beneficial results of the Mission were never so forcibly seen as during the *Forty Hours' Devotion*, which was commenced with a Solemn High Mass on Sunday, the 29th May, and concluded by a Solemn Mass and Benediction on the Thursday following, the Octave of Corpus Christi. Nothing could exceed the fervour and piety of the devout multitudes of all classes in society, who constantly thronged the church during the continuance of this sublime and truly majestic devotion, and were most anxious, even the poorest of the poor, to testify their faith in, and their love to, the Most Holy Sacrament by making offerings of wax candles. The brilliant glare of countless wax lights, the silent eloquence of enraptured adoration, and the fervent enthusiasm of the constantly succeeding stream of pious worshippers, all combined to render this portion of the Mission truly grand and not easily to be forgotten.[13]

A missioner observed that in these areas of western Ireland, even with their widespread poverty, the people were better instructed in their faith than people of the same class in other parts of England or Ireland. This was attributed not only to the zeal of the clergy but also to the presence of religious teaching Orders such as the Presentation Sisters and the Mercy Sisters.

Protestant missionary societies

But it was not only Catholic Religious who were attracted to the famine-stricken places. Evangelical Protestants saw the widespread destitution as an opportunity to send teams of missionaries of their own, commissioned by what Rinolfi calls the '*Protestant Missionary Society* of England and Ireland', but was actually *The Protestant Association*, a society based in London with headquarters at Exeter Hall in the Strand, where its annual meetings were held. They came armed with cash collected by special appeals in Dublin and in England. With this money chapels and schools were built to teach Bible Christianity with a strongly anti-Catholic slant. They also distributed money and food to alleviate hunger—but also as a species of bribe.

The so-called *Society for the Irish Church Missions to Roman Catholics* had for some time been seeking to convert Catholics in the west of Ireland to Protestantism through the action of proselytisers—or at least to lure away their children by the provision of Bible schools.

Rinolfi comments, regarding their first mission in Galway:

> From the opening of the Mission many efforts were made to darken, if possible, the brilliancy of truth; challenges to the Missioners and clergy, handbills and placards most insulting to Catholic feeling, were circulated and posted all over the city, inviting the inhabitants to controversial lectures, in answer, it was said, to the sermons of the Fathers.

But whilst Protestants, as we have already observed, flocked to hear the sermons of the Mission, the wretched proselytising parsons could scarcely ever muster an audience surpassing fifty persons, whether Protestants or what they call converts; one night they had only thirty-nine, just enough to represent, as a local paper wittily observed, the poor *thirty-nine articles* of their creed.[14]

Needless to say, these so-called 'proselytisers' were alarmed at the advent of the Catholic missioners. One technique they employed, which was a nuisance to the missioners, was to issue a challenge to a public debate on articles of Catholic teaching which Protestants regarded as heretical or irrational. These invitations were invariably ignored by Rinolfi and his companions, who regarded the prospect of a public debate as unbecoming—a waste of time and energy; however, Rinolfi did sometimes invite the proselytisers to come and see him privately to avoid an unnecessarily confrontational exchange—but that offer was never taken up.

Occasionally, a Protestant pastor would clandestinely attend a mission sermon, taking notes with a view to creating mischief. If they were identified, they were sometimes chivvied out of the building by angry Catholics, and on at least one occasion the missioners had to intervene before violence was inflicted on the intruder.

Inevitably, some Catholics had been seduced into joining up with the proselytisers, usually in order to get free education for their children. These were referred to as 'Jumpers', but the numbers were very few. However, in order to solicit funds the leaders of the proselytisers would exaggerate the number of converts, so as to advertise the purported success of their campaign. For instance, the Protestant vicar of Tuam claimed that he had made ninety-three converts from Catholicism including a priest, and published this as a fact in Dublin and Belfast to meetings of his supporters.

He was challenged to attend a meeting in Tuam, chaired by two arbiters, one Catholic and the other Protestant. The Vicar was unable to give the names of any converts, let alone ninety-three, and certainly no priest. Those who troubled to read the press report of this meeting would have realised that the Vicar's assertions were 'all humbug'.[15]

In various places, the missioners were approached by Jumpers who wished to 'jump back' and be reconciled. In Boyle, in the diocese of Elphin, there were some sixty of these Jumpers who came to Rinolfi after the close of the mission and, having begged forgiveness, Rinolfi reconciled them with the Church. When there was a similar cluster during one of the earlier missions, Rinolfi put together a simple liturgy of public reconciliation performed in the presence of the whole congregation.

During the Boyle mission Rinolfi observed that in no case 'was a Catholic found to connect himself in any way with these men [the proselytisers], but through extreme poverty or some other worldly motive—not in one single instance was any found to have yielded or continued with them through any sort of conviction'.[16] In other words it was human weakness that caused some to follow the Protestants and not through conscientious persuasion or any conviction that they were right.

Another canard put about by the proselytisers to explain the vast crowds who attended the missions was that 'if our Missions had produced any favourable impression, it was only on the minds of the poor and ignorant, whilst they were heartily despised by men of sense and literary attainments'. On the contrary, Rinolfi maintained, 'faith and genuine piety have, with very few exceptions, as great a hold on the minds and hearts of the rich and learned in Ireland as of the poor and illiterate'.[17]

The recipients of the missions were always loud in their praise and gratitude to the preachers. For instance, the people of Ballaghaderreen wrote to him:

You have preached what the founder of Christianity preached, what the Church taught, and still teaches; and the Bible, which we are told [by the proselytisers] is sealed against us, was your textbook. You have taught us to respect the conscientious opinions of those who differ from us, and to pity and pray for them, rather than condemn, while you have justly warned us against the designs of those men with honied lips, but poisoned hearts, who traffic in religion, and who would fain make their eternal salvation subservient to temporal happiness.

The sublime mysteries of our holy religion—a paradox to the unbeliever—when expounded in your truly simple but magnificent language, strengthen the Christian in his faith, and show forth at once the power and majesty of God, and the littleness of man. By that beautiful institution, the Sacrament of Penance, to which you have invited us, those who live in hate are now taught to love one another, and the nominal Catholic, who would try to reconcile conflicting views, is forced to receive truth in its entirety, or ignore Christianity altogether.[18]

The reception that Rinolfi and his fellow Rosminians received in Ireland was wonderfully warm and enthusiastic. And perhaps for that very reason it caused some evangelical Protestants to react even with violence in order to disrupt or counter the good that was being achieved by the missions. But it should emphasised again that by no means all Protestants were hostile. On the contrary, many attended the missions to hear and to learn, and were delighted at the effects the missions had on the general Catholic populace. And some of them were even received into the Church either during or after the mission.

It was a curious fact that hostile Protestant pastors singled out Lockhart for special attention, because he was a convert. A story was put around that Lockhart had publicly lamented that both his Protestant parents were 'damned and in hell'.

Lockhart repudiated this as absurd, as well as malicious, since his father had died when he was a child and his mother was still very much alive, indeed had followed him into the Church and was now a Catholic nun!

At Boyle especially, the Protestant pastor and his allies bombarded Lockhart with the charge that he had once subscribed to the 'truth' of the Thirty-Nine Articles but now repudiated them, and challenging him to debate these issues publicly, either face to face or through the press. Lockhart was a learned man, who throughout his life preached and wrote with theological foundation and conviction. However, he always dismissed the idea of a public debate with evangelical Protestants as pointless, a waste of time and energy, more inclined, he said, to inflame 'religious bigotry and party spirit' than to reach any form of consensus.[19]

The Rosary Procession

At the conclusion of a very successful mission in the picturesque town of Westport, Rinolfi, accompanied by another Rosminian priest, Fr Vilas, went north along the coastline of Clew Bay to the tiny village of Louisburgh. Nearby is the hill of Croagh Patrick, where St Patrick is reputed to have spent many a Lent and which is still a famous site of pilgrimage in Ireland.

There had been extensive depopulation here because of the famine and their expectations for the mission were not very hopeful. To their surprise, however, great numbers of people arrived from far and wide so that the services and talks had to take place in the open, from a specially erected platform.

In that area the proselytisers had been particularly active, and they had established a colony at Bunlahinch, about six miles out of Louisburgh. There they had built a small Protestant church and cottages to house the Jumpers. At the conclusion of the Forty Hours' Devotion, Rinolfi called up anyone who had been converted by the proselytisers and some thirty-five came forward. They were released from all censures, formally reconciled and invited to receive the sacraments of the Church along with the rest of the congregation.

Rinolfi proposed to the people that there should be a special procession of reconciliation to the colony. Taking a leaf out of St Dominic's book in dealing with the Albigensian heretics, the procession would pass through the settlement of Bunlahinch, publicly reciting the rosary for the intentions of the remaining Jumpers as well as for their 'captors'.

So, on the following Thursday a great procession over a mile in length was lined up and, headed by Fr Vilas on horseback, proceeded on foot through the colony reciting their beads in a very orderly manner. They assembled in a field close by the settlement, where a platform had been put up for Rinolfi to preach. Some magistrates then appeared along with the police seeking to prevent this public demonstration lest it cause a breach of the peace. But Rinolfi reassured them that no such thing would happen: the intentions of the people were entirely peaceful and that since the site was Catholic land they were within the law in using it for a religious occasion.

During his homily Rinolfi did not hesitate to condemn publicly all those Protestants from Henry VIII onwards who had tried to overthrow Catholicism. However, he was careful to distinguish between the proselytisers and the many sincere and upright Protestants who wished to live at peace with Catholics. They then prayed for all those in the colony who had seemed to turn their backs on their traditional faith, at which point another ten Jumpers came forward to seek reconciliation.

During their time at Louisburgh Rinolfi and Vilas, in the company of the local parish priest, visited Clare Island, which lies in the Atlantic between the mainland and Achill Island. Prior to the famine there had been some 500 families on the island, but that number had been reduced to only fifty or sixty, many of whom had already come ashore to attend the mission.

But the priests were conscious that others had been unable to travel, and it was primarily for their sake that this trip was made. The proselytisers had attempted to get a foothold on Clare Island but failed miserably.

A reasonable number of people turned up to hear Rinolfi preach an eloquent sermon on charity. Had he not known that they were fervent Catholics, he said, he would have deduced it from the evident love they bore to one another: 'they show they are Christians by their love'. When it came time to leave, it started to rain heavily but that did not deter the crowd from accompanying them to the boat waving their hats and handkerchiefs.

These missions to the west took place over three years, starting with the Galway mission in November 1852. During 1853 there were six missions; another six in 1854, and seven in 1855. In 1854 Rinolfi joined up with the Archbishop of Tuam, John McHale, in a sort of pilgrimage through the diocese when, as well as preaching in new parishes, they also revisited places where he had given a mission the previous year while the Archbishop conducted a round of confirmations. Rinolfi found that the rekindling of people's faith during the missions was still bearing fruit a year or more later.

On 2 July 1854 Rinolfi and Vilas started a highly successful mission in Ballinrobe, a town some fifteen miles from Westport. Once again the missioners observed in the people 'a most wonderful faith; a most undying devotedness to the Catholic Church; a most burning thirst after the Word of God, and after the fountains of eternal life'.[20]

Sadly, there occurred a most alarming incident on the first Thursday of this mission. During the night thieves broke into the church and stole sacred vessels and furnishings from the altar. They even took a ciborium containing the Blessed Sacrament. The people were horrified; Rinolfi responded by preaching on the words of the angel to Mary Magdalen at the tomb: 'Woman, why are you weeping? ... Because they have taken away My Lord and I do not know where they have laid him' (John 20:33). During the homily the tabernacle was left open and empty.

However, Rinolfi took the opportunity presented by the theft to celebrate the devotion of the people to the Blessed Sacrament by starting the Forty Hours' Devotion with a solemn outside procession finishing at an elaborately decorated altar. Fortunately, beautiful summer weather graced this occasion. The crowd that assembled was huge: 'scarcely less than fifteen thousand human beings of every age and rank prostrated themselves in adoration'. Thus, Rinolfi succeeded in turning a sacrilegious action into an opportunity for bringing a special blessing on the local people, while at the same time he wisely deflated any risk of a public backlash.

Later the Archbishop came to attend the mission and led another procession of the Blessed Sacrament as well as giving confirmation to over 500 people. Meanwhile fifteen or sixteen priests attended each day of the mission to hear confessions. On the final day, the feast of Our Lady of Mount Carmel, there was yet another procession for the opening of the new convent in the town to be staffed by the Sisters of Mercy. This mission to Ballinrobe was one of the most memorable of all the Rosminian missions in Ireland.

Achill Island

The concluding mission, preached in the west during 1854, was on Achill Island, and it was expected that this would be a challenging venture, because the proselytisers had been active there for some years even before the famine—for seventeen years in all—under the leadership of a Protestant churchman, the Rev. Edward Nagle. One year over 70,000 pounds had been expended in the island by the *Protestant Missionary Society*. Some twenty-two schools were established to lure the Catholic children away from their faith, chapels were built and a colony established, so that even some Catholic people were of the opinion that Achill had been converted to Protestantism.

However, the Franciscans had established a community on the island and the local Catholic clergy strove to preserve the people's faith. When Rinolfi and Vilas arrived on 30 July they were not confident of the same success as elsewhere—but they were happily proven wrong. From one end of the island to the other, large crowds arrived. The missioners found that of the twenty-two Protestant schools all but four had closed, and when they visited two of them they found just six children in one and only a single child in the other.

Nagle, though no longer an Achill resident, actively engaged in attacking the missioners, first issuing a challenge to a debate, which was ignored, and then distributing a scurrilous pamphlet, which the congregation tore into small pieces. Each day some of the Jumpers would return to seek reconciliation and readmission to the Sacraments, one day twenty, another day seventy, right up to the conclusion of the mission; this return of the prodigals continued for some weeks afterwards.

When, finally, Fathers Rinolfi and Vilas departed they were given a rapturous farewell by the priests and people. One local man wrote to *The Tablet*:

> the Mission of Fathers Rinolfi and Vilas in this island has shaken to the very foundation that accursed system which has been supported by the wealth and patronage of English zealots.

> The death-knell of proselytism in Achill has tolled. Numbers who flocked from the Colony and the prose-lytising schools to hear the words of wisdom which fell from the lips of those pious and exemplary Missioners, were reconciled to the Church, and returned home asking pardon for their sins, ... The far-famed Colony of Achill, the stronghold of proselytism in the far West, is almost a deserted village. Parson Nagle has fled in despair ...[21]

An article in the *Mayo Telegraph* rhapsodised over the influence Rinolfi and his companions had had:

> the sensation created by this extraordinary divine in this part of Ireland is quite remarkable. Wherever he went, thousands upon thousands followed in his footsteps; not only in the parish where he preached, but from other and remote places did the people repair to hear him again and again. No one could hear him—not the most hardened in sin—without profiting from his stupendous eloquence, so plain, so warning, so cogent.[22]

Rinolfi himself makes this comment regarding the infidelity of some:

> It would be a perfect miracle, if, after lavishing so much money—not thousands, but millions, those merchandizers of souls had not succeeded, in the midst of a famishing, a dying population, to find some poor wretches ready to sell their souls rather than die. The wonder is … that there are so few Jumpers in Ireland.[23]

And again,

> it is to be expected that when poverty, oppression, landlord intimidation and persecution seem to give a shadow of justification, at least to flesh and blood, for yielding to a course of outward apostasy and hypocrisy, men should be found ready to sacrifice their consciences, as well as those of their children, for a time. …

> The boasted success of proselytism has just had the effect of rousing both clergy and people to a deeper sense of the duty which they owe to religion, to remove, as far as is possible, every temptation of seduction from the Catholic poor, and to provide them with schools and other religious institutions …[24]

Conclusion

Rinolfi was to return to the west of Ireland from his base at Rugby the following year for another series of seven parish missions. Even after he was made Provincial in 1855 he still managed during the following twenty years to cross the Irish Sea regularly and build on what he and his companions had already achieved. In all, he was to preach over fifty parish missions in Ireland as well as giving many retreats, notably to the clergy.

His achievement, even his name, has been largely forgotten. Such, though, was his eminence during this page of Irish history that had his life ended in 1860 instead of 1877, there would surely have been some permanent memorial erected to him. In fact, the true and lasting heritage of Angelo Maria Rinolfi counts for far more than a statue or a memorial plaque. It lies in the thousands of people who heard him, and whose hearts and minds were moved and converted and greatly strengthened in faith through their encounter with him and his companions. Undoubtedly, the Catholic communities of today in the west of Ireland are the descendants and heirs of these thousands of people.

Irish Catholicism has had a quality over the centuries rich in simple piety, in a strong sense of justice, in a glorious survival against the onslaught of persecution, and in many missionary vocations. Even if the clergy scandals of recent times have militated against this wonderful tradition, one can look back on those Rosminian missions in the mid-nineteenth century as furnishing a unique contribution to a truly magnificent history.

NOTES

1   Hill, *The Rosminian Mission, Chapter 4.*
2   *Missions in Ireland, 1855, p. 17.*
3   *Ibid.,* p. 39.
4   *Ibid.,* p. 57.
5   *The Belfast Mercury,* 15 April 1851, quoted in *Missions,* pp. 43–4.
6   *The Drogheda Argus,* quoted in *Missions,* pp. 181–2.
7   *The Tablet,* 23 September 1854, quoted in *Missions,* pp. 326–7, with 'the judgement' changed to 'death and judgement'.
8   *Missions,* pp. 334–7.
9   *Ibid.,* pp. 67–8.
10 *Ibid.,* pp. 109–10.
11 *Ibid.,* p. 87.
12 *Ibid.,* p. 72.
13 *Ibid.,* p. 141.
14 *Ibid.,* p. 73.
15 *Ibid.,* pp. 134–6.
16 *Ibid,* p. 145.
17 *Ibid,* p. 147.
18 *Ibid.*p. 163.
19 *Facts of the Visit to Boyle of the Fathers Rinolfi and Lockhart ...,* 1853.
20 *Missions,* p. 238.
21 *Ibid.,* p. 292.
22 'Divine' was then commonly used to describe a priest or person in religious life.
23 *Missions,* p. 311.
24 *Ibid.,* pp. 313–14.

1. Monte Calvario, the Rosminian noviciate at Domodossola, Piedmont, where Rinolfi was received on 21 November 1834.

2. *Prior Park, Bath: the Mansion (right) and St Peter's College. Rinolfi lived here from October 1837 to July 1842, and taught in St Peter's College, Bishop Baines's secondary school for boys.*

3. St Mary's, Loughborough. St Mary's was the first Rosminian parish in England. Rinolfi was parish priest here from 1843 to September 1847.

4. Mount St Bernard, Leicestershire: the Calvary erected by Ambrose Phillipps. Rinolfi was present at the opening ceremony, presided over by Fr Aloysius Gentili, on 3 May 1843.

5. St Marie's, Rugby. As Provincial of the English Province, Rinolfi resided in Rugby for more than twenty years, and after his death in 1877 he was laid to rest in the churchyard of St Marie's.

6. Fr Aloysius Luigi Gentili (1801–48). The pioneer and leader of the
Rosminian Mission to Britain, Gentili's career was cut short when on
a mission to Dublin in 1848 he contracted typhus and died there.

7. St Nicholas of Myra, Francis Street, Dublin (parish of St Nicholas Without), where, in May 1850, Rinolfi held his first mission in Ireland. The church was a large one, capable of holding 3,000. The spire, which Rinolfi would have seen, has since been replaced.
(Dublin Penny Journal, *1832*)

8. St Malachy's, Belfast. Rinolfi, accompanied by Fr Lockhart, held a mission here during Holy Week and over Easter 1851. So large were the crowds that a second church, St Patrick's in Donegal Street, was needed to accommodate them.

9. St Mary's, Newport, where Rinolfi was parish priest from September 1847 until July 1849.

10. *Fr William Lockhart (1820–92). An early Tractarian, Lockhart was the first of Newman's circle to convert to Catholicism. He accompanied Rinolfi on numerous missions.*

11. *Fr William Lockhart (left) and Archbishop Manning (administering the pledge) at a temperance rally held on Clerkenwell Green, London, on 6 October 1872, mainly for the benefit of working-class Irish Catholics. Lockhart had previously addressed the gathering on the evils of drink. The public house on the corner in the background, The Crown Tavern, is still there.* (The Graphic, *19 October 1872*)

12. Fr Angelo Maria Rinolfi's grave in the churchyard of St Marie's, Rugby.

7

RINOLFI AS PROVINCIAL

IN JULY 1855 Antonio Rosmini died. Pagani and the other presbyters (priests who in those days formed the college of electors for a new Provost General) made their way to Italy for the election of a successor. Rinolfi should have been with them, since he had been made a presbyter a few years earlier. But as we have seen he was summoned to appear in court in Derry where some of the trouble makers from Newtown Limavady were being charged, and he was a key witness.

At the election Giambattista Pagani was chosen to be the second Provost General of the Institute, and one of his first actions was to appoint Rinolfi to be his successor as Father Provincial in England. When the electors returned to Rugby a few weeks later, there was a ceremony to install him into his new office. He was to remain Provincial for twenty years, retiring in 1875.

This new office now became his prime responsibility, and preaching missions and retreats came second. Nevertheless, in the years up to 1865 he was still preaching on average nine missions a year (compared with twelve or thirteen when he was a full-time missioner). As time went on, however, he preached fewer and fewer, probably because the work of giving missions was being supplemented by other congregations such as the Passionists and Redemptorists. Perhaps his responsibilities as Provincial took more of his time—or his energies were diminishing with age.

During the six years when he was missioning full-time, Rinolfi had undoubtedly accomplished much towards the revitalisation of faith in large numbers of people and he had become well known in England and Ireland. It is as well for us to take a pause and reflect on our knowledge of him. We know a lot about his achievements, but what of him as a person? What does he reveal about himself?

The short answer is very little, at least directly. In his writings he says practically nothing about his feelings and what it was that motivated him. In company he was a man of few words, even though his eloquence as a preacher had become legendary. And we should not forget that his own formation as a Religious would have moulded him in the virtue of humility so dear to Rosmini, always placing himself at the service of others.

In his book *Missions in Ireland* he quotes the comments in the press about the success of the missions and the qualities of the preachers, including himself. Huge crowds were attracted. The book refers to the 'hundreds', and indeed sometimes 'thousands' who flocked to hear him, and who continued to attend to the very end of the mission. There are many favourable comments sometimes in detail on the contents of his sermons and on the liturgies. There are also ample references to the conversions brought about by these missions.

Occasionally, he speaks of unusual events, such as the Protestant who seeks conversion because Rinolfi's preaching had caused an evil spirit to be driven out of him! And there are a couple of comments on sudden deaths of men who either refused to attend the mission or resisted the summons to conversion of heart. These are reported rather simplistically as 'wonders', whereas we may well see them as coincidences.

State of the English Province in 1855

During the previous six years while Rinolfi was preoccupied preaching missions often in faraway places, the English Province had been attracting a steady stream of vocations and was therefore expanding its works. Ratcliffe College was being built during the 1840s and the first pupils arrived there in 1847.

For a time it also functioned as noviciate and house of studies, and the community was always the biggest in the province. Augustus Welby Pugin, the celebrated architect, had proposed an ambitious quadrangle of buildings, and this expansion proceeded steadily after Pugin's early death under the eye of another architect, Joseph Hansom. The cost of this building was to be one of the headaches for the new Provincial. The quadrangle was eventually completed in 1860.

As we have seen, the first Rosminian parish in England (at Loughborough) was entrusted to the Order in 1841, and Rinolfi himself was one of the first to go there. A few years later Bishop Walsh offered the Rosminians another parish, at Rugby, close to Birmingham. Rugby in those days was a small market town, made famous during the nineteenth century by a flourishing public school, which today occupies much of the south side of the town. The school had for its headmaster a renowned educationalist, Dr Thomas Arnold: it was also the setting of a well-known Victorian novel, *Tom Brown's Schooldays*, published in 1857.

A wealthy Catholic family, the Washington Hibberts, who lived at Bilton Grange just outside Rugby, had been responsible for the purchase and development of a fine site alongside Rugby school on the Dunchurch road. The Hibberts had befriended Gentili, and it was probably through Gentili's influence that the husband, Captain John Hibbert, became a Catholic. Once again, Pugin was brought in to build a small church, eventually enlarged and completed in 1864 by his son Edward. The church, St Marie's, with its soaring spire is one of the finest Victorian buildings in England and remains in the care of the Rosminians to this day.

The first priests to arrive in Rugby, in 1849, were Pietro Bertetti and Moses Furlong. The Rosminians also built a formation house on the site, and the novices and students were moved there from Ratcliffe in 1852. The Hibberts continued to support the growth of the facilities, building both boys' and girls' primary schools, the latter being staffed by Rosminian Sisters much to the delight of Mrs Hibbert. Four Rosminian Sisters arrived in Rugby to take charge of the new school in 1855. The school flourished, developing a secondary college for girls as well.

Rinolfi used Rugby as his base during his twenty years as Provincial, and at various times he filled in both as parish priest and novice master. But it was south Wales that was to become the main focus of the Rosminians' pastoral activity. We have already noted Rinolfi's early involvement in the town of Newport. The continued Irish immigration caused Bishop Thomas Brown, who greatly admired the Rosminians, to call on them also to supply priests for the rapidly expanding town of Cardiff.

The first Rosminians to go there, in 1854, were both Italians, Fortunato Signini and the recently ordained Stefano Bruno. These two were to spend the major part of their priestly lives in Cardiff. Eventually the Rosminians were to run three large parishes, and Signini is remembered especially for the building of schools. Indeed, he was called 'the Father of Catholic schools'. When he went to Cardiff first there were none; when he retired twenty years later there were 2,000 children in Catholic schools in the town. Bruno is remembered not only for his zeal as a pastor but also for his skill as a peacemaker.

Later, Cardinal Wiseman of Westminster invited the Order to come to London, and in 1854 William Lockhart was sent to found a new parish in Kingsland, an inner suburb of North London. Lockhart was a great friend of Wiseman's successor, Henry Edward Manning, and they joined together regularly as temperance campaigners. Manning was eventually to give the Rosminians a central parish near the City of London, for which Lockhart acquired a neglected mediaeval chapel in Ely Place.[1]

These were the works whose care Rinolfi inherited. But with a regular stream of vocations, he was also able to respond to new invitations. One of these was running so-called 'industrial schools'. We may think of them as orphanages, or borstals, or remand schools. No boy was there by choice. The concentration of poor Irish immigrants in the industrial cities was one cause of widespread delinquency among the young, and these schools sprang up to deal with such problems. The aim was to care for these poor victims of neglect and poverty, to train them and prepare them for a healthy normal life as adults.

In 1857 two of these foundations were accepted by the Rosminians as pastoral works: one in the north of England at Market Weighton near York; the other in southern Ireland at Upton, outside Cork. The success of these foundations owed a lot to the wisdom and effective leadership of the priests appointed to be their directors: the jovial and energetic Carlo Caccia in Yorkshire and the highly experienced educationalist Moses Furlong at Upton. These two schools continued under Rosminian care until well into the twentieth century.

Two more such foundations were of shorter duration. In northern France there was a school set up by a French Rosminian, Fr Nicholas Lorrain. This continued until the outburst of anti-Church sentiment early in the twentieth century effectively drove Religious out of France. Also, for a very short time the Order took responsibility for a facility associated with Mount St Bernard's Cistercian abbey in Charnwood, Leicestershire.

The English Province decrees for 1861 indicate the extent of Rinolfi's charge. After twenty-six years the Institute had grown in numbers in Britain from the original three pioneers, Luigi Gentili, and the Frenchmen Antonio Rey and Emilio Belisy, to sixty-two professed members—thirty priests and thirty-two brothers. The largest community was at Ratcliffe College, with six priests and eleven brothers. Altogether there were five parish missions manned by thirteen priests; three industrial schools with two priests each, two priests at the students' house in Rugby and finally three priests who were itinerant missioners. The brothers were variously employed in teaching, looking after the young, and in manual labour such as running a small farm at Ratcliffe. There were fourteen Italians, four French, one Brasilian and forty-three English and Irish.

Rosmini had given his Institute the badge of universal charity, and the variety of works undertaken by the English Province during this period is a fine example of this principle put to practice. No one work or apostolate was to be preferred over another. Rather, each work asked of the Order was to be embraced with equal commitment, including an apostolate as daunting as the running of industrial schools, so long as the availability of men permitted.

Reviewing this history, the list of 'missions'—in the sense of apostolic commitments, and the numbers of men involved—provides us with a necessary introduction to the story of Rinolfi's life. But what was of greater importance for him as a Provincial was not the numbers or the occupations, but who these forty-two people were, how they lived and what they experienced. They were a group of men of different nationalities and vastly differing gifts. Some were barely literate coming from very humble backgrounds, others extremely talented as teachers or as preachers. But the common factor was that they were all human beings and Rosminians, and it was Rinolfi's job to know them intimately and to lead them in the way of service and holiness.

Hirst comments favourably on Rinolfi's virtues which fitted him for his new responsibility:

> During the time Fr Rinolfi held the office of Provincial, all who knew him can bear *witness* to the justice, charity and prudence of his dealings with his subjects. God led him on all occasions to act with justice according to the nature of the case. He could correct

firmly and strongly, but his corrections were always tempered with charity, and those who received them were obliged to acknowledge their justice …

He was full of charity, considerate for the feelings of others, entering into the smallest difficulties with fatherly kindness: the more needy the object, the more *overwhelming* was his charity. To some who knew him well and to whom he felt he could say anything without fear of being misunderstood, he often spoke abruptly and without any regard for their self-love; … [however] in the case of those who were timid and required some encouragement he was all kindness and gentleness. He was always prudent and reserved in his words, and all that he said showed his solid judgment and practical good sense.[2]

Though this encomium may be judged a piece of Victorian exaggeration, nevertheless, it has the authority of an eyewitness, Fr Hirst was almost his contemporary, and knew him personally.

Rinolfi was also noted as being himself a very observant Religious. When visiting a religious house he did not expect any ceremony, but simply slotted into the life of the community as if he belonged there, which in a sense he did. He was not only respected by his brethren: he was loved by them. Yet he remained throughout life a man of few words. He was a great listener, and perhaps that was what made him such an excellent Superior.[3]

Pagani, as we saw above, observed in a letter to Rosmini that Rinolfi 'has especial aptitude for remarking on the failings of others'. In other words, he was a good judge of people: he knew their shortcomings, but also their talents and virtues, and so would have been able to guide them in transforming any failings into something positive.

This may be illustrated by a document which Rinolfi drew up, presumably for Pagani, commenting on several of the leading members of the English Province at that time.

> *Moses Furlong,* Rector of Rugby parish, works away with much zeal and with genuine humility. He is a lover of religious discipline and is much attached to his vocation as a Rosminian. In exercising works of charity he displays a lot of patience and perseverance.

> *Carlo Caccia*, the Rector of the newly set up reformatory at Market Weighton in Yorkshire. This is a work of charity full of risk; nevertheless it has had singular and unexpected success, due to the qualities and attentiveness of this good priest. With all the activity this involves, he does not fail to show humility and piety.

> *Domenico Cavalli*. Rector of St Mary's Newport parish is a person of great good sense as well as religious spirit. He is prudent, and has at heart the best interest of the Institute of Charity. He has a very pure mind.

> *William Lockhart*. Rector of Kingsland parish in London. He is a convert from Anglicanism, showing commendable zeal in all he does. He is a gifted and eloquent preacher, a real asset for the people of Kingsland, but also for the many Protestants who come to hear him speak. He is very attached to his vocation as a Rosminian.

> *Nicholas Lorrain,* a Frenchman, is chaplain to the Phillipps family at Grace Dieu. He is a 'true Israelite in whom there is no guile'. He has the simplicity of a dove but also the prudence of a serpent. He too is very attached to his vocation, but tends to see himself as unworthy of it.

> *Fortunato Signini*, a missioner. He displayed much virtue when he was relieved of his office as Rector in Cardiff. His preaching on the missions is full of zeal.

These comments are commendably positive, and Rinolfi is simply paying tribute to the excellent team of Religious, who were running the major works undertaken by the Rosminians in England. However, he also had his problem subjects. The priest who had taken Signini's place as Rector in Cardiff was Lorenzo Gastaldi, a strong character and late vocation, who came to the Institute after being Rector of a seminary in Piedmont. One of the great tasks he accomplished was the building of the parish church of St Peter's, Roath, in Cardiff.

In Cardiff he had as one of his assistants another highly capable Italian priest, Giuseppe Costa. Initially, they made a powerful team, and the parish went ahead with great gusto. But then they fell out in a big away, to the extent that if one of them was in a room in the presbytery and the other came in, the first would immediately get up and walk out. Gastaldi eventually despaired of ever co-operating easily with his assistants, returned to Italy in a huff and left the Institute.

Costa stayed on in Cardiff for a time. He was greatly loved by the parishioners, but quarrelled incessantly with his fellow priests. If they said 'yes' he would, invariably, say 'no'. For instance Signini, who had returned as Rector, with the other assistant, Stefano Bruno, launched a campaign of moderation to tackle the very real problems of intemperance, especially among some of the poor Irish parishioners. Signini suggested that they should limit the amount of beer they drank to two pints a day for the men and one for the women!

Their advice was to some degree listened to and heeded, although the notion of rationing beer caused some amusement. But Costa would have none of it. For him it had to be total abstinence or nothing. Rinolfi became aware of the dissension among the priests, withdrew Costa and sent him back to Italy to cool his heels. In the absence of Costa, Signini and Bruno settled down and worked together harmoniously and effectively for many years.

By this time Pietro Bertetti, a former missioner in England, had succeeded Pagani as Provost General. Bertetti tried to interest Costa in the idea of going to America, responding to an invitation to send men. However, he did try one more time sending him back to England. He went first to Kingsland in London, but soon fell out with Lockhart, disapproving strongly of the way he conducted himself and the parish. So he returned to Cardiff, but nothing changed as regards his personal relationships. Eventually Rinolfi wrote in despair to Bertetti: 'What are we going to do with Costa? His conduct is such that he should be expelled from the Institute. But perhaps we should send him to America—on his own!'

Rinolfi's suggestion was accepted. Costa went to America and worked alone in the state of Illinois under the local bishop. Rosmini in his Constitutions had created the role of 'external coadjutor', a person who worked outside the Institute, yet still belonging and subject to the obedience of his Superiors. This fitted Costa perfectly. He flourished when he was his own boss. His parishioners were content to do what they were told without argument.

Indeed Costa was extremely successful in his ministry. He built up a wonderful parish in the Mid West in a town called Galesburg, Illinois. He would write regularly to Rinolfi pleading for someone to come and assist him. But Rinolfi always found an excuse: he knew it would create all manner of problems if he were to send assistants to Galesburg. Their correspondence remained friendly, and Costa often sent money back to help the English Province. The parish flourished under his zealous care. Eventually Costa mellowed with age, so reinforcements were sent. In this way Costa became the first leader of the American Rosminians, and he continued as parish priest until well into his eighties.

A very wise Rosminian once said that the one indispensable virtue of a member of the Institute of Charity was to be 'liveable with'. Rosminians are team people. Unless you can learn to live at peace and work in harmony with your brethren, how can you preach and teach charity to others? Rinolfi himself was an essentially a 'liveable-with' person and he fostered this trait among the brethren. Creating community was always a priority in his work as Provincial, and first and foremost he did it by humble example.

NOTES

1 See page XX.
2 Hirst, *op. cit.*, pp. 78–9.
3 See Hill, *The Rosminian Mission*, p. 247.

8

1855–1860: PAGANI AS PROVOST GENERAL

RINOLFI'S LIFE AS Provincial was quite different from the long periods when he had been exclusively a missioner. Although he preached fewer missions and retreats, his travels were by no means diminished as he criss-crossed through England from his base at Rugby visiting the various places where the Rosminians were working. For twenty years his manner of life would follow this pattern, so it is a continuous narrative. Like St Paul he was consumed by his 'anxious care for all the churches'. However, for the sake of convenience, this part of the story will be divided into sections according to who held the position of Provost General at the time: first Giovanni Battista (Giambattista) Pagani (1855–60), then his successor, Pietro Luigi Bertetti (1861–74) and finally Giuseppe Gioacchino Cappa (1874–77).

Rinolfi was an assiduous correspondent, and beginning in 1855 letters flowed from his pen to the new General Pagani, firstly at Stresa and then at Rome, after the household of the General had moved there. Fortunately, both Pagani and Bertetti had themselves spent many years on the English mission so they were basically familiar with the geography and the personnel. Pagani returned to England on visitation several times during the five years he was General.

Rinolfi knew him well since Pagani had been his immediate Superior from the very first year he had spent in England; therefore his letters tend to be a scatter of facts, requests and reports in no apparent order. They were like scribbled minutes.

There was no small talk, just information. One can imagine that many of them were dashed off by candlelight late in the evening, when Rinolfi was busy preaching a mission in the west of Ireland or in industrial Lancashire.

These were years of dynamic growth and, as is inevitable, of some trials too. All over the province there were buildings being extended or erected, land acquired and therefore money needed. In 1855–6, during the Pagani's first year as General, Rinolfi reports on schools in Newport and Cardiff, convents to house the Sisters, and the extension of Ratcliffe College. Then there were the personnel: brothers who were sick, novices who were being admitted or dismissed as unsuited to the religious life, and concerns about the health of the Sisters in Loughborough. A brother who was causing difficulties was clearly a victim of mental illness and needed to be sent for treatment—but, since he already belonged to the Institute, Rinolfi, in a fatherly manner, decides he was to be cared for within the Rosminian family, and not dismissed.

The new parish in London was a particular concern for the new Provincial. Kingsland was a growing inner suburb in north London, where there was neither church nor parish house. And in the neighbouring area of Hoxton there were a great many poor Irish immigrants. The new parish would provide work for two or three priests, and they of course had to be housed. Initially, the main church was a converted factory which the parish priest, William Lockhart, bought. His mother and sister were living close by, and they helped with finance. Lockhart himself was due to receive a considerable benefaction from the family estate, so he was able to borrow money with the confident hope that this bequest would enable it to be repaid.

Lockhart's sister was something of a special problem because she was busy founding a congregation of nuns to minister to the poor of Greenwich, in south-east London. It was not going well, and Lockhart was unhappy and preoccupied with what was happening to this project. So concerned was Rinolfi he intimated to Pagani his feelings that Lockhart's vocation was endangered. The greatly gifted Lockhart decided to make a retreat, and duly arrived at Rugby. It was Rinolfi's earnest hope and prayer that his vocation would be strengthened enough to cope with these family problems. Fortunately this prayer was heard, and the crisis blew over.

There were concerns also in Rugby about the Hibberts, who had given generously for the founding of the new parish of St Marie's and for the schools. As was often the case with English Catholic gentry, they thought the priests should be at their beck and call. Mrs Hibbert expected one of them, Fr Richardson, to be her personal chaplain, and this was neither good for Richardson nor for the blossoming parish, which could ill afford to give up a priest for an individual's exclusive needs. These concerns demanded exquisite tact on the part of Rinolfi as Provincial, especially since he was living in Rugby close by the Hibberts. He managed to detach Richardson without offending them.

South Wales was another paramount preoccupation, but here it was not the personnel—the crises over Gastaldi and Costa were things of the past—but challenges arising from the exploding growth in numbers of Catholics, largely due to Irish immigration. Rinolfi's first visit to south Wales was a very happy event, and he was able to send Pagani a glowing report. The two parish priests, Domenico Cavalli and Fortunato Signini made their presbyter vows,[1] and Rinolfi observed how highly they were regarded by the people. But there were pressing demands to build churches, presbyteries and schools, all of which meant raising a lot of money.

Concerning Signini, he writes: 'Truly the diligence, zeal and intelligence that Signini expends on the affairs in Cardiff gives me great hopes, even if he is lacking in domestic order and regularity'.[2] He was ably assisted by Stefano Bruno, who Rinolfi described as 'a fine missioner and an excellent religious'. They formed an admirable and stable team; this was just as well since in the early years Signini was often called away to preach parish missions, usually in the company of Rinolfi.

Signini was also most active in founding new schools. He was a great advocate of Catholic education, seeing it as a way of raising the status of the poor, especially the Irish immigrants. Interestingly, the state contributed £720 to build the parish school at St Peter's, while the parishioners contributed over £500 pounds. Rinolfi also mentions that they raised money by running a raffle, which strikes quite a modern note.

One issue that Rinolfi passed on concerned the Benedictines, who were planning to open a house in the city. Originally Bishop Brown had assigned the country areas inland to the Benedictines and the coastal strip to the Rosminians. It may be that Rinolfi thought Cardiff was not yet big enough to need the presence of a second religious Order.

As we have noted above, this period also saw the acceptance of a new charitable work, the running of so-called industrial schools. Most of the children in these schools were consigned to them by the local authorities. Hirst's biography contains an interesting account written by another Rosminian, Fr William Lewthwaite, who, like Lockhart, was a convert from High Church Anglicanism. He came from Yorkshire, where he had been instrumental in bringing the Rosminian Sisters to run a school at Clifford.

It was at Market Weighton near York that the first Industrial School was accepted by the Institute. Lewthwaite notes that an Act of Parliament had been passed setting up these schools, specifically acknowledging the claims of Catholics and other denominations to run their own. This was the first time in English law that the claims of denominational schools were officially accepted and recognised.[3]

Previously, invitations to found industrial schools had been in Ireland, specifically in Dublin and Belfast. Rinolfi explored these possibilities but did not accept them. For the Order to take on these works it was important that there be solid local support and funding. Bishop Briggs had already set up a small reform school, with extensive grounds, at Market Weighton, and in March 1857 the Bishop and his committee asked the Rosminians to take it over. Lewthwaite writes:

> The Provincial summoned his consultors to Rugby, and a meeting was held to take the proposal into consideration. They resolved to enter into correspondence with the committee, submitting to them various stringent conditions as terms for our acceptance of their proposal. The committee agreed to them all, and things being so far advanced, the matter was submitted to Rt Rev Fr Pagani, who gave it his full approval, and the undertaking was finally accepted. The Rev Charles Caccia was appointed to take on the management of the school, and with Brs Richards, John Bell, Bolger and Mulchen, arrived at Market Weighton on 1 June, when the responsibilities of the establishment were transferred to the Institute. There were 27 boys then in the school, but the accommodation was found in many respects very deficient for both masters and boys.[4]

Fr Caccia moved swiftly to establish the place properly to meet a much greater demand for places. A plan was drawn up to accommodate 120 boys, and by the end of 1858 the buildings had been completed at a cost of £4,000. By 1860 the school had grown to accommodate 200 boys. In 1863 Caccia also persuaded the committee to build a chapel, completed in that year.

This was felt to be a very great boon indeed, as not only could the service of the church be carried out more conveniently, but the refectory and adjoining room were set free for the use of the staff, which had been very much increased to meet the needs of the school.[5]

In 1860 the industrial school at Upton outside Cork in southern Ireland was accepted. It got off to a slow start and after a year there were only fifteen boys and a staff of eight. However the St Vincent de Paul society in Cork soon recruited more boys for the school and by 1862 there were 131 pupils. Fr Moses Furlong was put in charge, and he proved to be an effective head. His aim was to give his young charges a rounded education, teaching them to read and write as well as acquire skills for agriculture. He also brought music and drama into their curriculum.

The so-called 'delinquents' were kept very busy from dawn to dusk. But they were contented and gave very little trouble. Furlong was also determined that on release they should not return to the inadequate backgrounds that most of them had come from, and he arranged gainful employment for them. Many joined the army, and some went abroad, where Furlong organised contacts who would keep an eye on them as they settled into a new and independent life. Furlong proved once again to be a wise and efficient educator.

This success, along with the other industrial schools, has its source in Rosmini's teachings on the philosophy of the person. Education, for Rosmini, is a project of formation of the whole person, not just the teaching of individual subjects. So for Furlong and Caccia, the goal of integrating their student into society and the world of dignified work arose from an understanding of them as individuals in need not just of knowledge but personal guidance and practical assistance too.

In 1862 one of the brothers on the staff at Upton, named Wagstaffe, became very critical of his fellow staff members and even of Furlong, to the extent that Rinolfi was forced to take Wagstaffe away. He then proceeded to Dublin and laid a strong complaint against Furlong with the Director of Reformatories, urging that Furlong should be removed from office. Rinolfi tried to reason with Wagstaffe, but to no avail and he left the Institute. Rinolfi's comment regarding the state of Upton is revealing. Writing to Lockhart he says: 'From my own observation and information I have received the reformatory is by no means in a bad condition but the reverse.[6]

A third school was also initiated, this time in northern France, and the Frenchman, Fr Nicholas Lorrain, was sent as Rector. Established with the oversight of the Archbishop of Cambrai, the new school at Sainghin occupied a former sugar refinery, a building large enough to have the religious house, the reformatory and the orphanage all under one roof. Lorrain held the post of Rector and Novice Master until his death in 1873. The school was closed and the community withdrawn at the time of the outburst of anti-clergy sentiment in 1905.

All these ventures demanded the constant care and overview of Rinolfi, who visited the schools as often as possible to support the Rosminian staff and observe progress in this difficult apostolate. Initially he was quite concerned and, writing in 1862, characterised their general progress as only *'mediocremente'*—passable or tolerable. However, by 1866 he was entirely satisfied by the way they were run.[7] The diligent labours of the staffs were bearing fruit.

Rinolfi writes at least monthly to Pagani, often sharing concerns regarding some of the more troublesome brethren. Fr Mitchell in Cardiff had caused a scandal with his excessive drinking, and there was a move among the brethren to have him dismissed from the Institute. Rinolfi consulted the General and Mitchell was given another chance.

In 1860 Caccia reports of dissension among the community at Market Weighton with Fr Maxwell the chief culprit. Rinolfi counselled Caccia to give the brethren greater liberty, but Caccia reported this only made the situation worse! Rinolfi opted instead to take Maxwell with him as a missioner and so get him out of Caccia's hair.

A couple of religious who were incapable of maintaining discipline in the schoolroom had to be found places elsewhere. There were worries over property in Rugby and a crisis in

Loughborough with the convent drains, which resulted in serious flooding after heavy rain. All these concerns taxed Rinolfi's patience and industry while at the same time the variety of worries and struggles became the platform upon which Rinolfi exercised his leadership with prudence and care.

In 1859 he received two more serious offers for new apostolates. One was to take over a property near Dundalk in north Ireland which had belonged to an aunt of Furlong's. The thought was to purchase it as a mission headquarters for Ireland. Rinolfi went to inspect the property and reported that it was a fine house with twenty acres of land and a walled garden.

The other offer, which looked very promising, was an invitation from Bishop Ullathorne of Birmingham to take over the parish mission in Oxford from the Jesuits, who wished to withdraw. Rinolfi consulted various brethren, and Gastaldi and Lockhart in particular were keen for the Rosminians to accept: it could be a fertile source of good vocations.

Ostensibly these two offers were very attractive. But the demands of the existing parishes and the schools were considerable. Furthermore, Rosmini had been very specific in the Constitutions of the Order that no existing works should be abandoned in order to take on something more appealing. Dutifully then, Rinolfi had to decline both offers even though they might well have yielded benefit to the Order itself.

Another drain on his resources of manpower was the appointment of the Brasilian Cardozzo Ayres to become Bishop of Pernambuco in Brasil. Cardozzo had been spiritual director at Upton and was described as a very 'virtuous priest', but Rinolfi had some misgivings about his suitability for this new task. He was slow and indecisive and 'could scarcely put four sentences together'.[8] Another priest had to be taken away from Cardiff to act as the new bishop's secretary, so Rinolfi himself stood in as parish priest for a few months. He often tended to fill in gaps himself rather than disturb other works by taking people away who were well settled in an apostolate. In fact, it is noticeable that, with his keen eye on the apostolates themselves, he would leave men for a long time in each appointment, rather than move them frequently, as Pagani had been inclined to do.

The day after Christmas 1860 Pagani died unexpectedly. He was only 54, and although there had been no reports of any illness, his health had never been robust and he suffered from depression. This was a shattering blow to many of the English Rosminians who had for many years greatly respected and loved Pagani as a wise and gentle Superior. For Rinolfi it was the close of a long and fertile friendship, since Pagani had been influential in inspiring Rinolfi's vocation as a member of the Institute of Charity, and their respect for each other further grew over the years when one was Provincial Superior and the other Provost General. Another era in the life of the Institute closed.

NOTES

1   A fourth vow made by senior priests promising special obedience to the Holy See.

2   *Letter dated 23 November 1855.*

3   Hirst, , *op. cit., p. 83.*

4   Hirst, , *op. cit., p. 83.*

5   *Ibid., p. 85.*

6   *Letter dated 2 October 1862.*

7   Hill, *The Rosminian Mission, p. 259.*

8   *Letter of January 1860.*

9

1861–1874: BERTETTI AS PROVOST GENERAL

AFTER THE SUDDEN death of Pagani, Rinolfi, along with the other presbyters in England, went to Italy to elect a successor. He was Pietro Bertetti, a priest who had himself spent a few years on the English mission. Indeed he was the first priest to serve the Rosminian parish at Rugby in 1849. Later he was in charge of the scholastics when they were moved from Ratcliffe to the new college built in 1853 on a site next to the parish church in Rugby.

One person whom Bertetti came to know well was William Lockhart: they became good friends and Bertetti influenced him to take an interest in Rosminian philosophy. This was to bear fruit in later life when Lockhart studied and wrote about Rosmini's works. However, Bertetti's time in England was cut short when, in 1854, he returned to Italy to become the Procurator General of the Order. His job was to represent Rosminian interests to the Vatican.

His election as the third Provost General of the Order took place in January 1861. The first of Rinolfi's many letters to the new General was written from Stresa in February, before returning to England. It concerned another 'problem child', a Br Fitzgerald, who had been behaving scandalously and appeared to be 'out of his mind'. Should he be dismissed or sent to some institution for treatment?

By this time the attacks on Rosmini of the early 1850s had been settled by the intervention of Pope Pius IX and a decree clearing Rosmini from all suspicions of heresy or unorthodoxy.

Consequently, the flow of vocations in England and Ireland recovered for a time (as can be seen by the figures given above in Chapter 7).

In his letters to Bertetti, Rinolfi continued to employ the highly personal style he had used with Pagani, for Bertetti too was thoroughly familiar with English conditions and with many of the personnel. Rinolfi typically enters into quite minute details when speaking about proposed physical changes in the various properties. For instance, in September 1861 he writes about proposed alterations at Rugby where, alongside the parish church and schools, a college had been built in 1853 to accommodate the noviciate and scholasticate.

Evidently Bertetti had made a visitation there recently, and proposed that the noviciate be moved into separate premises. Rinolfi goes into meticulous details for carrying out this plan: how should the coach house be altered? how many rooms were there and how many Religious could be accommodated? where was the kitchen to be? how could the garden be kept private from casual visitors? where might the itinerant missioners stay when they returned to base? And, perhaps most importantly, how much would it all cost?

Rinolfi had always had an eye for detail including the somewhat awkward need for financial support of the Order and its works. In his book *Missions in Ireland*, he had described an occasion in Clifden where the people were so delighted with the work of the missioners that they spontaneously collected a large sum of money for training future Rosminians. It is also clear from his correspondence that Rinolfi was shrewd in sending out gift copies of his book, with the suggestion that a donation towards the upkeep of the Rosminian formation houses would be greatly appreciated. No aspect of management and planning, however trivial, escaped his eagle eye to become part of his dutiful reporting of events to the General.

However, his letters to Bertetti contain much more than the details of buildings and costs. There is the business of who is to be placed where, so that the Order's works of charity could go ahead as well as possible. An instance of this is his concern for Furlong's health. The mission in York had left him exhausted and unwell. How would he cope when he was sent to be in charge of the new school near Cork? Rinolfi speculates that the Irish climate might be better for him—and so it proved. Furlong flourished there.

> Then there is the brother who cannot keep discipline in the primary school at Rugby: where to move him to? A new rector will be needed in Rugby, having responsibility not only for the parish but also for the community in the new college. The right man seems to be a new Italian, Fr Castellano.

These are all details of leadership management—property management and personnel guidance and appointment. But what weighed most on Rinolfi's shoulders as Provincial were brethren who did not get on with each other or were unhappy under a particular Superior. Foremost among them was Giuseppe Costa, whom we met in Chapter 7. He had shown great promise as a young Religious and was prefect of novices and then of scholastics. He excelled in leadership, though today we might describe him as a 'one man band'.

As we have seen, Costa was eventually sent on his own to America, where he was a highly successful parish priest of Galesburg in Illinois. He wrote cheerfully and regularly to Rinolfi, pleading for him to send more priests to help him: there was plenty of work to be done. But Rinolfi feared what might happen if he were to send reinforcements to work with him, and diplomatically pleaded that vocations were short and demands were great. In one letter to Costa he states:

> Do you know what? Cardozzo (the Brazilian) was consecrated Bishop of Pernambuco in Rome and Fr

Caccia is to go with him to Brazil next month, and who is to fill his place in Cardiff? Why, myself! So you see, in this year we lose four priests I may say. Fr Vilas dismissed, Fr Akeroyd disabled for work for eight months and perhaps forever after a railway accident. Msgr Cardozzo and Caccia gone to Brazil. You see there is no talk of purchasing colleges or embarking in anything else in England, America or elsewhere.

Taking on Cardozzo's place in Cardiff typifies Rinolfi's policy of filling an unexpected gap himself rather than upset the staffing of other works. He waited to fill the post until the next yearly decrees allocating works and personnel.

Missions and Retreats

Meanwhile Rinolfi continued his apostolate of parish missions and giving retreats. Between February 1861 and June 1869 he preached twenty-eight parish missions and some ten retreats, mostly to priests or religious communities. This activity was less frequent than in earlier times because of the demands on him of being the Provincial. Rugby's central location in England made it a convenient base, and he travelled to the various missions easily by train.

Unfortunately, there are no records of the content of Rinolfi's sermons during these missions apart from some scanty references in the press (see examples quoted above). The list of his missions has a gap between June 1869 and February 1875. Another unfortunate deficiency is that although he has left summaries of his retreats and a few skeleton summaries of his sermons, no copies of the text of any of his sermons has survived. But this perhaps gives us a further insight into the man and priest. He preached not 'at' his congregation but 'with' and 'to' them, preferring a more engaging style. It may well be that he preached only from notes and not from a pre-prepared text so as to place the parishioners at the heart of his encounter with the Word of God and themselves.

However, we do know that he habitually preached from scriptural texts, especially from the Gospels. His primary emphasis, like Gentili's, was on conversion of heart. In this respect they were both following the lead of Jesus himself, who began his public ministry with the famous challenge: 'Repent, and believe the Good News'.

The Scottish Jesuit Gerard Hughes, in his book on spirituality *God of Surprises*, gives an eloquent reflection on conversion of heart:

> When God, in Christ, says 'Repent and believe the Good News', he is uttering an invitation not a threat. It is as though he is saying to us, 'Come and see what I want to give you and you will find that it goes beyond your wildest dreams ... Come out of the prison of your tomb, break down the walls of your false securities, and come with me so that you and I can live as one undivided person'.
>
> Repentance is accepting this invitation; sin is the refusal to accept it ... Unless we repent we cannot discover the treasure ... Without repentance we become idolators of wealth, status, power, although we may still claim to be religious people.[1]

Those who attended these missions were undoubtedly religious people, in the sense that they were professed Catholics or Protestants. What they were all being challenged to do was to *repent*, to take a step further and undergo a change of heart. Those who came out of curiosity were called to embrace a life of commitment. Those who were routine Christians, perhaps a little lax in their practice, were invited to a life of more regular observance and holiness.

The Sacrament of Penance was a vitally important part of the Rosminian Missions, because it gave the penitent the grace to take this further step of conversion. The preachers prepared the people to receive the Sacrament by moral discourses, sermons on the Commandments, and the imperative to change their way of life. They were calling on their listeners to become open to the healing gift of divine forgiveness. The missioners themselves would spend long hours in the confessional, and usually they needed to call upon priests in the surrounding area to come in and help.

In those days most Catholics thought they needed to go to confession before receiving the Eucharist. So most of those who received the first sacrament went on to receive the Eucharist, often several times during the mission. At a time when frequent communion was rare, one of the fruits of the mission was to encourage the people to come to the altar rails more regularly.

During his early years as Provincial he was often accompanied on missions by Fortunato Signini; in March and April 1862 they were together in Scotland for three weeks during Lent at St John's parish in Glasgow. This city had been one of the main destinations for Irish immigration following the famine, and the numbers who came to the mission were overwhelming. Over 5,000 people received communion and there were 500 confirmations when the bishop attended. Signini commented afterwards: 'This mission was most laborious but it consoled us by the great fruit which it produced'.

Signini eventually became more and more involved in the labours of the Cardiff parish, so he ceased to help on the missions. Likewise William Lockhart was busy establishing parishes in London. In 1875 he was given another responsibility as Procurator General of the Order, which meant he had to spend several months of the year in Rome. At this time Rosmini's writings were again coming under attack, mostly from a group of Jesuits, and the work of defending the founder also fell on Lockhart's shoulders. Although unavailable for preaching missions, he was constantly in demand as a public speaker on temperance and other issues, right up to the time of his death in 1892.

The other great missioner, Moses Furlong, became completely engrossed with founding and running the reformatory at Upton in southern Ireland. In fact, as time went on the Rosminians were less frequently called upon to preach parish missions, and this work was taken over by other Orders such as the Redemptorists, the Passionists, the Jesuits and the Dominicans.

Rinolfi himself continued giving retreats right up to his retirement as Provincial and beyond, although he preached fewer missions. It was a time of consolidation for the English Province, and no new parishes were taken on. However, in London Cardinal Manning offered Lockhart a parish in Saffron Hill, more central than Kingsland and not far from St Paul's Cathedral and the City of London. This move took place in 1874, when Manning was Archbishop. Rinolfi noted that he was much more kindly disposed towards the Rosminians than his predecessor, Wiseman, whose antipathy had been influenced by the criticisms of Rosmini's writings in Italy.

Manning and Lockhart had been friends since they were both Anglicans and they worked together in London on social concerns, especially on temperance campaigning. Writing to the General, Rinolfi says that the Cardinal is 'gracious and friendly towards us'.[2] Lockhart was fortunate to acquire as the new parish church, St Etheldreda's, Ely Place. This beautiful mediaeval building in a quiet, gated cul-de-sac off Holborn, had once been the chapel of the palace of the Bishops of Ely in London: it remains in the care of the Rosminians to this day.

There is an interesting letter from Rinolfi from this late period of his time as Provincial (January 1872), asking Pope Pius IX for a special blessing for Fr Henry Clark, an English Rosminian and chaplain to the Marquess of Bute in Cardiff, who was seriously ill. In it Rinolfi also summarises the mission in Cardiff:

> The Rosminian mission is to the maritime city of Cardiff in South Wales, where there are 9000 Catholics scattered over a large district. There are two churches and three chapels and some ten Masses are said each Sunday.

But he does not mention the presence there of the Rosminian Sisters, teaching nearly 2,000 schoolchildren.

Rinolfi continued preaching a few missions and giving retreats, almost to the end of his life, though suffering from the effects of the diabetes, which triggered his resignation as Provincial in 1875. He kept in close contact by letter with Bertetti. This friendship, which he clearly treasured, ended with Bertetti's death in September 1874.

NOTES

1   Hughes, Gerard W., *God of Surprises*, p. 64.
2   Hill, *The Rosminian Mission* p. 260.

10

FINAL DAYS

THE YEAR 1875 was crucial one in the life of Rinolfi. There was a new Provost General, Bertetti's successor, Fr Gioacchino Cappa. He had joined the Rosminians, along with Lorenzo Gastaldi, after Rosmini's works were placed on the Index of prohibited books in 1849. Both men had been shocked at the treatment Rosmini had received, and it induced them to join up. Cappa had never been on the English mission, so for the first time Rinolfi was reporting to a General unfamiliar with English conditions and who would have known only a few of the brethren in Britain.

A document which Rinolfi put together at this time listing all the properties which the Rosminians now held in England and Wales, was presumably intended to help the new General understand the detailed structure of the English Province. An example is the parish at Loughborough, which reads as follows:

> Loughborough. Diocese of Nottingham
>
> This was the first parish mission entrusted to the Institute in 1841 by Msgr Walsh. This mission owns a tract of land with an area of about 2420 square yards, on which were constructed the chapel, the parish house and a school ... This property is worth about 4000 pounds sterling.

Such meticulous detail would enable the General to envisage the extent and value of the various properties. Similarly, in his reports about people Rinolfi goes into rather more detail than he would have needed to do for either Pagani or Bertetti.

It was during 1875 that Rinolfi first began to show the initial symptoms of the diabetes which was eventually to take his life, and this manifested itself in increasingly defective eyesight. His writing becomes untidy and more difficult to decipher, and in one place he laments that he is unsure what he is writing because he cannot see the paper properly.

His condition continued to steadily deteriorate, and on 20 August he wrote to Cappa asking to be relieved of the duties of being the Provincial Superior on account of his failing vision. He was also facing the prospect of an operation to remove cataracts. Cappa took Rinolfi's request to heart and responded quickly, replacing him as Provincial with another Italian, Fr Gazzola.

He also mentions that Fr Bruno in Cardiff had suggested he move there, as the burgeoning mission in the city was in need of more help. As Provincial, Rinolfi had been based in Rugby, an ideal location for the Provincial's residence because of its centrality in England, but once relieved of those responsibilities he would be free to move to Cardiff, where he had worked for some months in 1868.

However, before vacating his office he had to deal with one last serious problem. In August he had been giving a retreat at Ratcliffe to the local clergy of the Nottingham diocese, when the new Bishop told Rinolfi that he wished to make an official visitation to the Rosminian convent in Loughborough.

Rinolfi responded by pointing out that the Rosminian Sisters were exempt from official episcopal oversight, and therefore the internal life of the convent was in fact under the supervision of a Director who was always a Rosminian priest. It happened at that time to be Rinolfi himself. It would not therefore be proper for the bishop to undertake this role, as any notion of dual direction might cause possible conflict and confusion. Rinolfi put this to the bishop quite forcefully in a letter:

> I beg to thank your Lordship very sincerely for your
> kind favour. I am glad you have not yet written to

Rome, but I am sorry at the same time that you still contemplate doing so under certain circumstances. I enclose a copy of the letter in question, kindly requesting that Your Lordship return it to me after perusal.

I cannot name any convent of nuns in England subject to a religious Superior and not to a Bishop. But if there was no other convent in England, the case would be much stronger in favour of Loughborough Convent, since the decision of Propaganda Fide would actually regard only that convent, which was in existence before 1868, though it was made general and embracing all convents of nuns under Religious Superiors that might be in existence before that date…

I have not the least doubt of your Lordship not having any right to visit this Convent. For I cannot view that document in any other light than confirming its exemption from Episcopal Visitation, which it had before practically enjoyed. …

In face of the decision alluded to, I admit that no new foundation of a central house of our Sisters can be made in England unless a declaration be made, *in limine fundationis*, between the General of the Institute of Charity and the Bishop of the Diocese in question, that the Sisters are establishing their house according to their Rules and Constitutions as belonging to the Institute of Charity and enjoying exemption. With this understanding alone was the central house established at Loughborough. And if that original understanding is to have no more force, I see nothing but a dissolution of the Community looming in the distance with all its scandalous consequences and intricacies of vested rights accumulated over the space of thirty years …

You see, My Lord, the question is a very vital one, and if solved according to Your Lordship's views, it must sooner or later bring about what Your Lordship I am sure does not wish, the disbanding of the present

Sisters of the Institute of Charity, and render it impossible for them to be established again in England. For a double jurisdiction over them could never be reconciled, and the Father General could never think of standing in opposition to a Bishop; it is one of our principles of the Institute to pay all deference to the wishes of the Bishops of the Church and to serve them in every way.

Your Lordship will excuse me therefore if I repeat that if the Propaganda is appealed to for an explanation, in the sense proposed by Your Lordship, this ought to be done by the united action of the English Bishops, as it was by such a united action that the Decree was obtained. I would then beg Your Lordship if you cannot bring yourself to drop it altogether, to let it stand over until the Bishops can meet, or till the next Westminster Synod in 1876. Then the Bishops will be able to discuss the matter fully and decide accordingly.

This masterful letter, written towards the end of Rinolfi's life, reveals much about his character. Though humble in disposition he would not be deterred from defending justice and what is right. The disagreement was over the matter of governance. The bishop was of course welcome to visit the Sisters informally.

The 'letter in question' which Rinolfi refers near the start was the original document from Propaganda Fide in Rome setting up Loughborough Convent as being clerically exempt from formal episcopal visitation. The convent, which was the Mother House of the Sisters in the province, was to be overseen by the Fathers of the Institute of Charity and not by the local bishop.

The masterstroke of Rinolfi's diplomacy was to turn the disagreement away from himself by urging the bishop to share his intention with all the bishops of England. Rinolfi wagered that the thought of presenting the proposal in that context might check the bishop's resolve!

The bishop replied evasively, but was not prepared to concede Rinolfi's argument. So Rinolfi responded on 10 November 1875, putting his case again with utmost clarity:

> In the hope that your Lordship has not yet written to Rome, I beg to take the liberty to express the surprise your letter of last night caused me and I don't wish one day to pass without begging your Lordship to reconsider the matter. The decision of Propaganda seems to me *very* plain. The question was about the dependence of Nuns subject to Generals of Religious Orders on the Bishops, so that the Bishops could visit them and give them directions as they do to Nuns immediately subject to themselves. The decision, if it means anything, means independence or exemption from episcopal jurisdiction and visitation. Such from the first was the interpretation put upon it by the English Bishops up to the present, who have carefully abstained from interfering with the Convents (in existence before 1868) subject to the Generals of Rel. Orders.
>
> In any case, as the decision was obtained (and is applicable to all Convents subject to Rel. Superiors) by the body of the English Bishops, it seems to me that no single Bishop should apply for an explanation of it, but this should be done by the united actions of the English Episcopate and consequently your Lordship should consult with the rest of the Bishops and act together and then give all the Convents under Religious Superiors the chance of standing or falling together.

The dispute seems to have been settled amicably: the Rosminian Sisters continued to enjoy the episcopal clerical exemption which had been granted them from Rome, and nothing more was heard of the matter. But it was no longer Rinolfi's direct concern, since he had now retired from being Provincial.

His health continued to deteriorate and with it, his stamina. That he was no longer physically capable of continuing the life of an active missioner can be seen from a letter written after a mission in Manchester undertaken at the end of 1875 in the company of Fathers Lockhart, Smith and another priest. He writes that it was 'a very laborious mission, and I feel rather knocked up'. For the first time in twenty-five years Rinolfi admits to physical weakness.

This was the fourth of his beloved missions that he gave during 1875, the others being in Coventry, Nottingham Cathedral and Stockton-on-Tees. He also preached three retreats that year. But it was clear that the time for him to retire from such an active ministry was fast looming.

During the following year he travelled to London to have the cataract operation, but it did not give him much relief. Diabetes is a serious condition affecting the whole body and particularly blood circulation to the limbs; before the discovery of insulin, it usually shortened the life of the sufferer. During the final year of his life Rinolfi spent much of this time on parish work in Cardiff. This must have brought him satisfaction as the various works of the Order in Wales were vibrant and engaging. There, he preached his final public sermon on Christmas Day 1876.

Then he returned to Rugby, where his health rapidly deteriorated. He was unable to celebrate public Masses but would say a votive Mass of Our Blessed Lady every day, which was all that his failing eyesight allowed. He celebrated this Mass in a temporary oratory which had been set up next to his room, since he could no longer manage the stairs. He continued to do this under the care of his brethren, right up to the last day of his life.

On 20 February 1877 he died at the age of 64. His well-attended funeral took place in the parish church on 23 February: the Bishop of Birmingham presided and Fr Lockhart preached a funeral oration. Rinolfi was buried in the graveyard on the south side of the church. In the course of time the tombstone became covered with moss and lichen, and its location was lost. Indeed, until lately records stated that he had died and been buried in Italy. His grave has recently been rediscovered, the inscription (revealed by cleaning) indicating it to be the final resting place of Fr Angelo Maria Rinolfi.

Rinolfi was a very humble Religious, and the fact that the only known public memorial of his noble life is in the church at his birthplace, Prato Sesia, is a testimony to one who sought no honours for himself, but simply to serve God by living and proclaiming the Gospel. His true memorial was in the hearts of his brethren who loved him and in the minds of the thousands who were moved to repentance and change of heart by his preaching. After his death the London *Tablet* had this to say about him:

> As a sacred orator Fr Rinolfi had perhaps few equals in his day. With a real and deep earnestness of soul, a doctrine always correct and solid, a logical closeness of reasoning, … a diction as simple, easy, and appropriate as it was expressed in a clear, sonorous voice, and accompanied with a natural pleasing gesture; he so mastered his hearers that when the peroration came, every one felt, as even the preacher felt, convinced of the eternal truth announced, and impressed with the necessity of surrendering to its sovereign claims. Not to speak of innumerable other places, all the larger towns of England, Ireland and Scotland experienced the fruits of his missionary labours.

> But while speaking of him as a most successful missionary, we do not by any means place in this the principal merit of his life. What seems to us much more important is that, esteemed and admired as he knew himself to be, he was a very unassuming and humble man. He spoke very little, and never about himself or his doings. In fact, he was very diffident about his own powers, and always feared lest he should be producing more harm than good. Hence proceeded his great reserve when having to pass a judgment on anything. And, on the

other hand, it was this very humility and caution, joined with his well-known good sense that caused his advice in matters of difficulty to be much sought by those well-acquainted with him. ...

In his capacity as Provincial the chief characteristics observed in him were great charity for his brethren, no matter whether priests, clerics or lay-brothers, each of who seemed to feel that in him he had a father and a friend; also prudence and discretion to an exquisite degree, which enabled him to combine together, to the satisfaction of all, an unswerving firmness of purpose to keep all steadily to the end of their holy vocation, with gentleness in the way of his doing so.

In a quiet, simple way his life seems to have been ruled by this one principle, 'Do the will of God as pointed out by your sphere of duty in the best manner you can, and forget your own feelings and convenience for the sake of charity'.[1]

The principles which Antonio Rosmini gave to his followers are beautifully exemplified in this tribute from *The Tablet*. Humility was always to the fore in Rosmini's mind. He saw humility as the highest of the virtues and the gateway to wisdom,[2] and the 'foundation of the whole life chosen by us'.[3] Angelo Maria Rinolfi was an exemplary Rosminian; he loved his vocation, and all the years of his adult life he lived it to the full. In him the ideals of Blessed Antonio Rosmini are completely personified.

NOTES

1   *The Tablet*, 3 March 1877, p. 275.
2   See *Introduction to Philosophy*, 67.
3   *The Constitutions of the Institute of Charity*, C521.

11

THE EVANGELISER

ORATORY AS AN art is as old as civilisation. It predates the discovery of writing and the beginnings of literature. The orator was the one who passed on to succeeding generations the wisdom of the tribe, the history of the people, and the legends and poetry of their culture.

In New Zealand this can still be seen in the traditions and ceremonials of the Maori people. On the *marae*, the meeting place of Maori tribes, visitors are welcomed by oratory; problems are brought to a solution by debate; the history of the Maori people, the settlement of the country and their strong religious beliefs are passed on by the elders of the tribe. The young are obliged to listen and learn so that in their turn they too will be able to transmit the collective wisdom of the people to future generations.

The survival of these ancient Maori customs is by no means unique: it is to be found among many ancient cultures, especially when undisturbed by the arrival of European or other migrants. Before people were able to appeal to or consult written documents, they had to rely on the usually trustworthy memories of the wise ones of the tribe, who were the guardians of tradition and culture.

Even in European history the names of the great orators of the past are recalled and honoured. Demosthenes of Athens in the fourth century B.C.is remembered as a Greek states-man—but even more so as an orator. In Celtic tradition the *bard* filled the role of story-teller and proclaimer of the history of the people. This tradition of bardic eloquence is to be found at Welsh cultural gatherings, known as *Eisteddfodau*, and continues to flourish among famous Celtic statesmen like the great Irish patriot, Daniel O'Connell, and the Welshman and one-time Prime Minister of Britain, David Lloyd George. During World War II, Winston Churchill used his mastery of the medium of radio to raise the spirits and courage of the British people with rousing and colourful broadcasts. His successors had to master the arts of television as well as radio, while more recently politicians and communicators have had to come to terms with the whole gamut of different opportunities now available in the age of digital technology and social media.

It is necessary to distinguish between *orators* who persuade their audiences by argument and by empathy—of whom a contemporary example would be Barack Obama—and *demagogues* who mesmerise their audiences, already preconditioned into an attitude of hero worship. Both Hitler and Mussolini were orators of this genre. A friend of mine went to hear Mussolini declaiming in the Piazza Venezia in Rome in 1938, and although he detested everything Mussolini stood for, he said he had to make a conscious effort not to join in the rapturous applause. He felt seduced by the insidious influence of the demagogue.

Clearly the preacher is in a different category from all the above examples; nevertheless, he or she too will utilise many skills shared by all orators: voice projection, gesture and clarity of speech, as well as ways of winning and holding the attention of the audience. But it is important to emphasise that the basic task of the Christian preacher is to evangelise—to bring people to Jesus Christ and to the Gospel. He or she must be more than simply an orator.

Down the ages many great preachers have etched their names in Christian history: Bossuet and Fénelon, for instance, in eighteenth-century France, and the great Dominican Père Lacordaire in the nineteenth. In England, John Henry

Newman had a unique ability to hold a congregation in thrall, especially in his Anglican days when Vicar of St Mary's University church in Oxford. Many Anglican clergymen were educated at Oxford and their thinking and spirituality were profoundly influenced by Newman's sermons.

So, what is it that makes a great preacher? Evidently, the content of the sermon is of primary concern. Karl Barth, the eminent Lutheran divine, insisted that preachers had to be theologians: 'as theologians we ought to speak of God. People seek us to help in the dilemma of God's existence. What they cry out for is not *a* truth but *the* Truth. It is a cry not for a solution but for salvation'.

The word 'salvation' prompts us to acknowledge that the listener must be disposed to hear, indeed, must be anxious to receive the Good News. What the preacher is striving for is not just to inform the mind but to transform the heart of the person in the pew. To achieve this, his message will need to be relevant to the life of the hearer. It must be in context. It has been said that the preacher should have the Bible in one hand and the daily newspaper in the other. The preacher is essentially an evangeliser.

Rinolfi, as we have seen, was a highly successful missioner and retreat giver. He had the advantage that he was not simply preaching once to his congregation, but over and over again during the weeks of the mission. The attendees would be receiving a succession of homilies, and therefore, over an extended period, the process of transformation could occur gradually. It is for this reason that there were so many converts during these missions. It is quite likely that a person would look back on the mission many years later as a time of great grace, a time when they truly heard the voice of God.

When Jesus preached in Galilee he was revealing to the people the message of the Father. His cry was 'Repent!' In other words 'change your hearts; convert your souls'. And for this to happen there must be more happening within the hearer than simply absorbing beautiful words. There will need to be the presence of the Holy Spirit receiving the Word and transforming the hearer. It is like a sacrament. The presence of God becomes real in the heart of the believer.

An American Protestant writer lists the characteristics of a good homilist as follows:

1. The sermon must *confront* the listener: it must invite change of heart.

2. It must *instruct* the hearer; it teaches Christian doctrine.

3. It must *reveal* to him/her the presence of God as found in Scripture.

4. Good preaching always demands long and purposeful *preparation*.

5. The sermon will engage the *doubts and fears* of the listener.

6. The preacher must not gloss over or minimise the *cost of conversion*.

7. (Preaching should arise out of the *personal experience* of the preacher: it relates the truth as the preacher has discovered it in his/her own life. The preacher must be authentic.[1]

We may note that Rinolfi's preaching ticked most of these boxes. His sermons were central to the process of evangelisation which is what these parish missions were all about. Rinolfi was not merely teaching and persuading. He and his companions were offering a whole package: they were introducing the people to the key sacraments of conversion; they were reminding the people of their baptismal obligations; they were appealing to the presence of the Holy Spirit in their hearts.

It was hoped that the congregation would accept these truths and take them to heart. It was more like a dialogue. They were engaging with the people, and the high point of that engagement would be in the sacraments of Reconciliation and Eucharist. The liturgy and the hymn singing would help to move the hearts of the people to joyful acceptance of the message. One who comes to church to receive God's word and to hear its application from the mouth of the homilist will hopefully gain a precious insight to apply to their own lives. It will help their growing awareness of truth and their personal growth in holiness. It is a work of the Holy Spirit dwelling in them.

Cardinal Newman took as his motto *cor ad cor loquitur*—'heart speaks to heart'. The heart of God utters the truth to be received by the human heart. Newman was primarily thinking of prayer, but he was also a great preacher: his sermons touched the young people, who hung upon his words in St Mary's Church in Oxford. Likewise this appeal to the heart was central for Rinolfi and his companions in their dedicated life of missioning.

One may imagine Rinolfi during his retirement recalling that interview he had had with his novice master at Rosmini's behest, when the prospect of going on the English mission was placed before him. He embraced it as his religious obedience, and he spent his life in a foreign land preaching God's word to thousands of people, rich and poor, ignorant and well educated, hungry for faith or simply curious. In his time of retirement therefore he could reflect on a vocation from God well spent.

NOTES

1   Honeycutt, Frank, *Preaching for Adult Conversion.*

125

APPENDIX

MISSIONS AND RETREATS

This list of Missions and Retreats undertaken by Fr Rinolfi between 1844 and 1876 is based on the Appendix to Hirst's *Words and Works of Father Rinolfi*, pp. 102–107 ('Missions given by Father Rinolfi'), with some additional information from local newspapers.[1]

Year	Month	Place	Mission	Retreat
1844		Loughborough, Leics	*	
		Shepshed, Leics	*	
1845	August	Nottingham (Sisters of Mercy)		*
1846	May	Hinckley, Leics	*	
	August	Birmingham (Sisters of Mercy)		*
		Melton Mowbray, Leics	*	
	September	Loughborough (Sisters of Providence)		*
		Atherstone, Warwicks (Sisters of St Dominic)		*
	November	Loughborough (Sisters)		*
		Ushaw, Co. Durham		*
1847		Birmingham (Sisters of Mercy)		*
		Ratcliffe (College Community)		*

Year	Month	Place	Mission	Retreat
1848	July	Oscott (Midlands Clergy)		*
	August	Loughborough (The Sisters)		*
		Ratcliffe (College Community)		*
1849	March	London, Southwark, St George's	*	
	July	Oscott (Midlands Clergy)		*
		Ushaw (York Clergy)		*
		Liverpool (Sisters of Mercy)		*
		Bishopstone (Lancashire Clergy)		*
	September	Manchester, St John's	*	
		Ushaw (Students)		*
		Bolton, Lancs, SS Peter and Paul	*	
	October	Bolton, St Mary's	*	
		Knaresborough, Yorks	*	
		Brewood, Staffs	*	
	November	Leeds, St Anne's	*	
	December	Grantham, Lincs	*	
1850	January	Whitwick, Leics	*	
		Ratcliffe (Students)		*
		Hull, Yorks	*	
	February	Sheffield, Yorks	*	
		Manchester, St Augustine's	*	

Year	Month	Place	Mission	Retreat
	March	Liverpool, St Mary's	*	
	April	Liverpool, St Patrick's	*	
	May	Dublin, St Nicholas's, Francis Street	*	
	June	Dublin, St Andrew's, Westland Row	*	
		Loughborough (The Sisters)		*
	July	Birkenhead, Cheshire	*	
	August	Wigan, Lancs, St Patrick's	*	
		Chorley, Lancs	*	
	September	York, St George's	*	
	October	Worksop, Notts	*	
		Rainhill, Lancs	*	
	November	Ampleforth College, Yorks		*
		Manchester, St Patrick's	*	
	December	Liverpool, St Peter's, Seel Street	*	
1851	January	Morpeth, Northum'd, St Robert's	*	
		Cowpen, Northum'd	*	
	February	York, St George's	*	
		Dublin, St Audeon's	*	
	March	Liverpool, St Joseph's	*	
	April	Belfast, St Malachy's	*	

Year	Month	Place	Mission	Retreat
1851	May	Thurnham, Lancs, St Thomas's	*	
	June	Atherstone (Sisters)		*
		Garstang, Lancs	*	
	July	Great Ecclestone, Lancs	*	
		Fleetwood, Lancs	*	
	August	Ushaw (Clergy)		*
		Keighley, Yorks	*	
	September	Stalybridge, Cheshire	*	
	October	Bolton	*	
		Lytham, Lancs	*	
	November	Liverpool, St Anne's	*	
	December	Manchester	*	
1852	January	Blackburn, Lancs, St Alban's	*	
	February	Coventry, Warwicks	*	
		Bath, St John's	*	
	March	London, Poplar	*	
	April	Liverpool, St Patrick's	*	
	May	Macclesfield, Cheshire, St Alban's	*	
	June	Dublin, SS Michael and John's	*	
	July	Loughborough (The Sisters)		*
		Rugby (Community)		*
	August	Loughborough (Ladies' Retreat)		*

Year	Month	Place	Mission	Retreat
	September	Salford, Lancs, Cathedral	*	
		Burnley, Lancs	*	
	October	Newport, Mons	*	
	November	Galway, St Nicholas's	*	
	December	Dublin, St Audeon's	*	
1853	January	Clifden, Co. Galway	*	
	February	Newry, Co. Down, Cathedral	*	
	March	Ratcliffe College		*
	April	Tourmakeady, Co. Mayo	*	
		Fairhill, Co. Galway	*	
	May	Headford, Co. Galway	*	
		Tuam, Co. Galway, Cathedral	*	
	June	Boyle, Co. Roscommon	*	
		Ballaghaderreen, Co. Mayo	*	
		Tuam (Clergy-1)		*
	July	Tuam (Clergy-2)		*
		Westport, Co. Mayo (Sisters of Mercy)		*
	September	Clifford, York	*	
		York (Convent)		*

Year	Month	Place	Mission	Retreat
1853		Chorley, Lancs	*	
	October	Drogheda, St Peter's	*	
	November	Glasgow, St Mary's	*	
	December	London, Southwark, St George's	*	
1854	January	Manchester, St Patrick's	*	
		Gravesend, Kent	*	
	February	Liverpool, St Mary's	*	
	March	Nottingham, Cathedral	*	
	April	Dublin, St Andrew's, Westland Row	*	
		Liverpool, St Joseph's	*	
	May	Castlebar, Co. Mayo	*	
	June	Westport	*	
		Louisburgh, Co. Mayo	*	
	July	Ballinrobe, Co. Mayo	*	
		Roundstone, Co. Galway	*	
		Clifden	*	
	August	Achill Island, Co. Mayo	*	
		Dublin (Carmelites)		*
		Newton Limavady, Co. Derry	*	
	November	Cardiff	*	

Year	Month	Place	Mission	Retreat
	December	London, Hammersmith	*	
		London, Clerkenwell	*	
1855	February	Liverpool, St Patrick's	*	
	March	Manchester, St Chad's	*	
	April	Glasgow, St Mungo's	*	
	May	Kilconla, Co. Galway	*	
	June	Errisanna	*	
		Partree	*	
	July	Rugby (Community)		*
	August	Mount Bellew, Co. Galway	*	
	September	Dunmore, Co. Galway	*	
		Claremorris, Co. Mayo	*	
	October	Wolverhampton, Staffs	*	
	December	Loughborough	*	
1856	January	London, Spitalfields, St Anne's	*	
	February	Stalybridge, Cheshire	*	
	March	Salford, Cathedral	*	
	June	Oldham, Lancs	*	
	July	Whitehaven, Cumberland	*	
		Loughborough (Sisters)		*

Year	Month	Place	Mission	Retreat
1856	August	London, Westminster (Clergy)		*
	September	Drogheda	*	
	October	Galway	*	
	November	Oranmore, Co. Galway	*	
	December	Liverpool, St Peter's, Seel Street	*	
1857	February	Dublin, St James's, St James's Street	*	
	March	Glasgow, St Andrew's	*	
	April	Edinburgh, St Patrick's	*	
		Dundee	*	
	June	Aldershot, Hants (Soldiers)		*
	July	Ratcliffe (Clergy)		*
	September	Newtownbarry, Co. Wexford	*	
	October	Rosnaree, Co. Meath	*	
	November	Stone, Staffs	*	
	December	Dublin, St Catherine's, Meath Street	*	
1858	January	Guernsey, Channel Islands	*	
	February	Dublin, St Paul's	*	
	March	Birmingham, Cathedral	*	
		Shrewsbury, Salop	*	

Year	Month	Place	Mission	Retreat
	April	Dublin, St Andrew's, Westland Row	*	
	May	Piercestown, Co. Wexford	*	
	July	Oscott (Clergy)		*
	October	Thurnham, Lancs	*	
		Scorton, Lancs	*	
	December	Drogheda	*	
		Banbury, Oxon	*	
1859	January	Market Weighton, Yorks		*
		Douay College		*
	March	Sheffield, St Marie's	*	
	April	London, Kingsland	*	
	May	Dublin, Rathmines. Our Lady of Refuge	*	
	June	Drogheda	*	
	July	York (Clergy)		*
	September	Swansea	*	
	October	Liverpool, St Mary's	*	
		Aberdeen (Blairs College)		*
	November	Durham	*	
	December	Gosport, Hants	*	

Year	Month	Place	Mission	Retreat
1860	January	Bolton	*	
	February	Dublin, St Paul's	*	
	March	Liverpool, St Joseph's	*	
	April	Drogheda, St Peter's	*	
	May	Navan, Co. Meath (Young Men's Society)		*
	June	Reastown, Co. Louth	*	
	November	Blackburn	*	
	December	Birkenhead	*	
1861	February	Douay College		*
	May	Cork (Blackrock Convent)		*
		Cookstown, Co. Tyrone	*	
	July	Loughlin Convent		*
1862	March	Nottingham, Cathedral	*	
	April	Glasgow, St John's	*	
	June	Portadown, Co. Armagh, St Patrick's	*	
1863	March	Liverpool, St Joseph's	*	
		Bradford, St Patrick's	*	
	May	Lurgan, Co. Armagh	*	
1864	February	Liverpool, St Anthony's	*	

Year	Month	Place	Mission	Retreat
	March	Warrington, Lancs	*	
1865	June	Donaghmore, Co. Tyrone	*	
1866	January	Selby, Yorks	*	
	March	London, Kingsland	*	
	April	Birmingham, West Bromwich	*	
	May	Ratcliffe (College)		*
		London, Poplar	*	
	June	Sedgley, Lancs	*	
	August	Birr, Co. Offaly (Sisters of Mercy)		*
	November	Birr (Young Men's Society)		*
1867	March	London, Spanish Place	*	
		Coventry	*	
	April	Newport, Mons	*	
	May	Liverpool, St Anthony's	*	
	August	Cork (Clergy)		*
		Newcastle, Co. Down	*	
	October	Drogheda, St Peter's	*	
1868	February	Cardiff	*	
	March	Liverpool, St Patricks	*	

Year	Month	Place	Mission	Retreat
1868	April	Market Weighton (Reformatory)		*
		Selby	*	
	May	Armagh, Cathedral	*	
	June	Banbridge, Co. Down	*	
	August	Dromore, Co. Down (Clergy-1)		*
		Dromore (Clergy-2)		*
	September	Bridgend, Glamorgan	*	
1869	April	Loughborough Convent		*
	May	Ratcliffe College		*
		Leitrim, Co. Leitrim	*	
	June	Ballymoney, Co. Antrim	*	
1875	February	Coventry	*	
	March	Stockton-on-Tees, St Mary's	*	
	July	Cork (Clergy)		*
		Loughborough (Sisters)		*
		Ratcliffe (Clergy)		*
	October	Nottingham, Cathedral	*	
	December	Manchester, St Augustine's	*	
1876	March	Mount St Bernard's (Reformatory)		*
		Liverpool, St Sylvester's	*	

NOTES

1   After the June 1869 retreat at Ballymoney the list from Fr Hirst's book is defective for the next five years; the list becomes accurate again after February 1875 Coventry mission.

BIBLIOGRAPHY

The principal source of information on Rinolfi's life and works is the Rosminian Archives, Collegio Rosmini, Via per Binda 47, 28838 Stresa, Novara, Italy.

Barth, Karl (tr. A Marga), *The Word of God and Theology*. Continuum, 2011.

Einaudi, Giulio (publ.), *Storia d'Italia*. Turin: 1989.

Handy, Francis, *Jesus the Preacher*. Abingdon-Cokesbury, Nashville. 1949.

Hill, J. M., IC, *Antonio Rosmini, Persecuted Prophet*. Leominster: Gracewing, 2014.

Hill, J. M., IC, *The Rosminian Mission*. Leominster; Gracewing, 2017.

Hirst, Joseph, IC, *Words and Works of Father Rinolfi. Provincial of the Order of Charity in England*. Market Weighton: St. William's Press, [c.1890].

Honeycutt, Frank, *Preaching for Adult Conversion*. Nashville: Abingdon Press, Nashville, 2003.

Hughes, Gerard W., SJ, *God of Surprises*. Darton, Longman & Todd, Ltd, 1985.

Leetham, C. R., IC, *Rosmini, Priest, Philosopher and Patriot*. Baltimore: Helicon Press, 1958.

Leetham, C. R., IC, *Luigi Gentili: A Sower for the Second Spring*. London: Burns & Oates, 1965.

Mariani, Domenico, *The Rosminian Generals and Bishops*. Stresa, Rosminian Editions, 2004.

Reclus, Élisée, *La Nouvelle Géographie Universelle, la Terre et les Hommes*. 1875.

[Rinolfi, A. M.], *Missions in Ireland: Especially with Reference to the Proselytizing Movement... By One of the Missioners.* Dublin: James Duffy, 1855.

Roscommon & Leitrim Mission, *Facts of the Visit to Boyle of the Fathers Rinolfi and Lockhart, Missionaries of the Church of Rome.* Boyle: J. Bromell, 1853.

Rosmini, A., *Epistolario Completo.* Casale Monferrato: Giovane Pane, 1887–1894. Complete letters in 13 volumes.

Rosmini, A., *The Ascetical Letters of Antonio Rosmini.* Translated and edited by John Morris, IC, and Donal Sullivan, IC. Loughborough: John Morris, 1993–2012. 8 volumes.

Rosmini, A., *Introduction to Philosophy.* Translate by Robert A. Murphy. Durham; Rosmini House, 2004.

Sagliaschi, Claudio, *Prato Sesia, Il Percorso Millenario di una Comunità.* Associazione Turistica Pro-Loco di Prato Sesia, 2014.

INDEX

13. Superior at Prior Park: 15–19. Phillipps's chaplain at Grace Dieu: 22–25. Parish priest at Loughborough 1842: 27–30. First Rosminian to preach public missions (1845–1848): 36, 39, 40. Death in Dublin in 1848: 52–56. Also 31.

Glasgow, W Scotland. Missions preached: 32, 110.

Grace Dieu, Leicestershire, home of Ambrose Phillipps: 22–23, 27–28, 90.

H

Hibbert, John Washington and family: financed the parish development in Rugby: 85–86, 97, 98.

Hirst, Joseph i.c. author of a biography of Rinolfi: viii, 8, 12, 42, 88, 89, 127.

Hughes, Gerard s.j. 109.

Hutton, Peter i.c. Became a Rosminian at Prior Park. Later President of Ratcliffe College: 30, 32.

K

Kingsland, N London: Rosminian parish founded by

Lockhart: 86, 90, 92, 96, 111, 135, 137.

L

Liverpool, Lancashire, N England: Rinolfi preached more than twelve missions in the city: 32, 34, 39, 45, 48–49.

Lockhart, William i.c. Disciple of Newman. Converted to Catholicism and became a Rosminian (1843): 23–24. Missioner and Rinolfi's companion: 34, 40, 47–48, 56, 59, 68–69, 73–74, 81; parish priest in London (1854–1892): 86, 90, 92, 96–98, 102, 105, 110, 111, 118.

Lorrain, Nicholas i.c. Rector of Sainghin Industrial school, N France: 87, 90, 101.

Loughborough, Leicestershire, English Midlands. First Rosminian parish in Britain. Rinolfi parish priest (1845–1848): 22, 25, 27, 30, 32, 56, 85 96, 102, 113, 116.

Louisburgh, Co. Mayo, W Ireland. Mission preached: 74–75.

M

Manning, Henry Edward, Cardinal Archbishop of Westminster. Friend of Lockhart and fellow temperance campaigner: 86, 111.

Market Weighton, Yorkshire, N England: Industrial school, presided over by Fr Carlo Caccia: 49, 87, 90, 98–99, 101.

Maxims of Christian Perfection, written by Antonio Rosmini (1830). The essence of Rosminian spirituality xii, 11.

McHale, John, Archbishop of Tuam: 76.

Milan, NW Italy: 7,8.

Missions in Ireland: book about parish missions conducted in Ireland, written by Rinolfi: viii, 38, 54, 51–83.

Monte Rosa, prominent Alpine peak visible across NW Italy: vii, 3.

Monte Calvario, Domodossola, N Italy. Rosminian novitiate. Now, mother house of the Institute of Charity: xii, 10–12.

Mount St Bernard's Abbey, Charnwood, Leicestershire. Cistercian monks from Ireland introduced by Ambrose Phillipps: 87.

Munthe Axel, Swedish writer. Author of *The Story of San Michele*: 43, 50.

N

Narchialli, Carlo i.c. Rinolfi's seminary and novitiate companion: 10, 11, 13.

Newman, John Henry (later Cardinal). Influential leader of the Oxford movement to Catholicise the Anglican church. After his conversion to Catholicism (1845) he became a friend and supporter of the Rosminians: 23–24, 31, 37, 56, 123, 125.

Newport, Monmouthshire, S Wales. Rosminian parish from 1848: 32–34, 36, 86, 90, 96.

Newtown Limavady, near Derry, N Ireland. Mission where Rinolfi and the attending people

formation in the Institute of Charity: 10–13; teaching at Prior Park: 15–21; parish at Loughborough: 23–30, parish priest: 30–32; Newport: 32–36: first missions: 37–49; missions in Ireland: 51–81; Provincial of the Rosminians in Britain: 83–112; final days and death: 113–118; tribute: 119–120.

Rinolfi, Lorenzo. Eldest brother of Angelo Maria, diocesan priest: xii, 4–5, 9–11.

Rosmini, Antonio. Founder of the Institute of Charity and first Provost General. Writer of *The Maxims of Christian Perfection*. Rinolfi's counsellor: xi, 11–13, 15–16, 19–22, 24–25, 30, 34–36, 39, 46, 64, 83, 88–89, 92, 102, 105, 113, 120.

Rugby, Warwickshire, English Midlands. Second Rosminian parish. Rinolfi's base as a missioner; he died there in 1877: 50, 67, 80, 84–86, 90, 97, 99, 101, 105, 106, 108, 118.

S

Sainghin, N France : Industrial school, headed by Fr Nicholas Lorrain: 50, 101.

St Etheldreda's church, Ely Place, London. Rosminian parish founded by Lockhart. He died there in 1892: 98, 111.

St George's, Southwark, S London. Mission preached: 34.

Signini, Fortunato i.c. Rinolfi's frequent mission companion: 1–2, 13, 15–18, 32–33, 35, 40; Parish priest in Cardiff and founder of Catholic schools: 86, 90–91, 97–98, 110.

T

Tablet, The. Catholic periodical published in London: 45, 62, 78, 119–120.

Tuam, W Ireland. Mission preached: 65, 71–72, 76.

Turin, NW Italy: 7, 8, 12.

U

Ullathorne, William, Bishop of Birmingham. Sup-